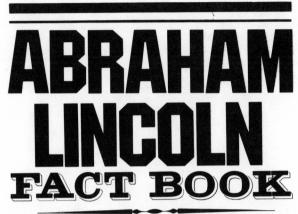

ABRAHAM LINCOLN FACT BOOK

& Teacher's Guide

by Gerald Sanders

EASTERN ACORN PRESS

PICTURE SOURCES: *Bridgeport Public Library* page 51 (top); *Chicago Historical Society* page 41 (top); *Henry E. Huntington Library* pages 11, 20; *Illinois State Historical Library* pages 1, 15 17, 21, 23 (center & bottom), 26 (top), 27, 35 (top), 40 (right), 56 (top); *Library of Congress* pages 16, 19, 22, 29, 30, 32 (top), 34 (top), 35 (center), 36, 42, 44 (top), 51, 56 (left); *Lincoln Memorial University* page 10; *Lincoln National Life Foundation* pages 34 (bottom), 50 (top); *National Archives* pages 40 (left), 46-7; *New-York Historical Society* pages 9, 23 (top), 49 (left & center), 50, 51, 55 (bottom); *New York Public Library* pages 14, 32 (bottom), 33, 35 (bottom), 37, 41 (bottom), 44, 45, 49 (top), 50 (bottom), 51 (bottom), 55 (top right); New York Times pages 52-54; *Louis A. Warren Lincoln Library & Museum* pages 18, 38 (top); *Western Reserve Historical Society* page 39 (bottom).

Eastern National provides quality educational products and services to America's national parks and other public trusts.

Sixth Printing, 1997

Copyright 1982 Eastern Acorn Press
Design by Winston Potter
Games courtesy of Lincoln Home NHS, Springfield, IL

Library of Congress Cataloging in Publication Data

Sanders, Gerald.
  Abraham Lincoln fact book and teacher's guide.

  SUMMARY: Presents the life, times and death of the 16th President.
    1. Lincoln, Abraham, Pres. U.S., 1809-1865—Miscellanea.
  2. Presidents—United States—Biography—Miscellanea.
  [1. Lincoln, Abraham, Pres. U.S., 1809-1865—Miscellanea.
  2. Presidents-Miscellanea] I. Title.
  E457.909.S26   973.7'092'4   [B] [92]   82-18781
  ISBN 0-89062-086-5 (pbk.)

Manufactured in the United States of America

Contents

An Abraham Lincoln Chronology

1806   Thomas Lincoln marries Nancy Hanks.

1807   Their first child, Sarah, born in Elizabethtown, Kentucky.

1809   February 12. Their second child, Abraham, born on frontier farm on Nolin Creek near the present Hodgenville, Kentucky.

1811   Family moves a short distance to Knob Creek. Abraham Lincoln attends school there.

1816   December. Family moves farther west to the present Spencer County, Indiana.

1818   October 5. Mother dies.

1819   December 2. Father marries Sarah Bush Johnston. Lincoln (age 10) gains stepsisters Elizabeth (age 12) and Matilda (age 8) and stepbrother John (age 9).

1821   June 14. Stepsister Elizabeth marries Dennis Hanks.

1826   August 2. Sister Sarah marries Aaron Grigsby.

        September 14. Stepsister Matilda marries Squire Hall.

1828   January 20. Sister Sarah dies.

        Lincoln helps take load of farm produce down the Mississippi River to New Orleans on a flatboat.

1830   Family moves to Illinois.

1831   Makes second flatboat trip to New Orleans; subsequently hired as a store clerk in New Salem, Illinois and settles there.

1832   Chosen captain of volunteer company in Black Hawk War (but sees no action).

1834   Elected to Illinois State Legislature; begins to study law.

1836   Receives license to practice as an attorney.

1837   Moves from New Salem to Springfield, Illinois.

1842   November 4. Marries Mary Todd.

1844	Visits former Indiana home while campaigning for Henry Clay, the Whig presidential candidate.
1847	Goes to Washington, D.C. as Whig congressman from Illinois.
1854	Seeks, but fails to win, nomination to run for the U.S. Senate.
1858	Nominated to run for the Senate and attracts national attention for the Lincoln-Douglas debates in unsuccessful attempt to defeat Senator Stephen A. Douglas.
1860	May 18. Receives Republican nomination for the presidency. November 6. Wins presidential election.
1861	February 12. Spends fifty-second birthday crossing Indiana on inaugural trip to Washington, D.C. March 4. Inaugurated as sixteenth president. April 12. Confederate bombardment of Fort Sumter marks beginning of Civil War.
1862	September 22. Issues preliminary proclamation of emancipation.
1863	January 1. Final Emancipation Proclamation declares that slaves "shall be . . . forever free." November 19. Delivers Gettysburg Address.
1864	November 8. Begins second term as president of the United States.
1865	April 9. Civil War ends at Appomattox. April 14. John Wilkes Booth shoots the president during a performance of *Our American Cousin* at Ford's Theatre in Washington, D.C. April 15. Lincoln dies at 7:22 A.M. May 4. Lincoln is buried at Oak Ridge Cemetery in Springfield, Illinois.

This drawing, with the caption "All Seems Well With Us," appeared in *Harper's Weekly* the day Lincoln died, April 15, 1865. The magazine had gone to press earlier; the words referred to the surrender of Lee at Appomattox. But Lincoln's death made them seem ironic.

Brief Life
of Abraham Lincoln

Born into a pioneer family, the man who became sixteenth president spent his youth and early manhood on the frontier.

When he was seven, Lincoln's family left their native Kentucky for a home in Indiana. His mother, Nancy Hanks Lincoln, died barely two years later, in 1818. The following year his father, Thomas, married Sarah Bush Johnston.

Lincoln received his education by attending occasional terms of school in Kentucky and Indiana. Accustomed to long hours of hard physical work at an early age, he found time for self-education by borrowing books and weekly newspapers. As a young man he traveled twice to New Orleans.

After his twenty-first birthday in 1830, the family moved to Macon County, Illinois. Soon Abe left his family and moved to New Salem, Illinois where he became a clerk and part-owner of a store with partner William F. Berry. His other jobs included postmaster and surveyor in New Salem. He ran for a seat in the Illinois state legislature in 1832, but service as a captain in the Black Hawk War prevented campaigning and he lost. He was later more successful politically and in 1834 was elected to the first of four terms in the Illinois legislature. It was from this beginning that Lincoln began to attract attention as a political leader.

In 1837 he moved to Springfield, Illinois, where he met Mary Todd, whom he married in 1842. The Lincolns had four sons, Robert, Edward, William, and Thomas, two of whom (William and Edward) preceded their father in death.

Lincoln served in the United States Congress from 1847 to 1849. He then spent five years building his Illinois law practice and gaining enough prestige to be mentioned as a vice-

"If any personal description of me is thought desirable, it may be said, I am, in height, six feet, four inches, nearly; lean in flesh, weighing, on an average, one hundred and eighty pounds; dark complexion, with coarse black hair, and grey eyes—no other marks or brands recollected."

Although he was recognized as a gifted orator, it was plain speaking that won Lincoln the popular support. Nineteenth-century advertisers often alluded to his honesty in support of their own claims. B. Leidesdorf and Co. named him as a patron of their chewing and smoking tobaccos.

presidential candidate at the first Republican presidential convention in 1856.

As an opponent of Stephen A. Douglas for the United States Senate in 1858, Lincoln participated in famous debates on the extension of slavery. Lincoln's speeches against slavery contributed to his prominence and ultimately won him the nomination for the presidency.

The Republican convention in Chicago nominated Lincoln in May 1860, and he defeated three other contenders in the November election.

By his inauguration on March 4, 1861, eleven southern states had already formed the provisional government which became the Confederacy. On April 12, hostilities began at Fort Sumter. Faced with civil war, Lincoln issued a call for troops, blockaded southern ports, and took other measures to prepare the country for a war to preserve the Union. Early military defeats took the northern states by surprise.

Lincoln issued a preliminary and conditional emancipation proclamation on September 22, 1862. On January 1, 1863 the formal and effective Emancipation Proclamation declared "all persons held as slaves within any State . . . forever free." Later in 1863, at the dedication of the Gettysburg, Pennsylvania battlefield cemetery on November 19, Lincoln delivered the Gettysburg Address. A third important Lincoln document of 1863 was the Thanksgiving Proclamation that formally established a major national holiday.

Politics and a successful military operation were the highlights of 1864. That year's political convention renominated Lincoln and selected Andrew Johnson, a Democrat, for vice president on the Union ticket. On March 4, 1865, in his second inaugural address, later called "the outstanding state paper of the nineteenth century," Lincoln promised victory for the North but assured charity for all. On April 9, 1865, General Robert E. Lee's Confederate Army surrendered.

On Good Friday, April 14, only five days after the Union victory, Lincoln was shot by an assassin in Ford's Theatre. He died at 7:22 A.M. the following day without regaining consciousness.

This undated photograph is generally accepted as an accurate picture of Lincoln's father.

The Lincoln Family

☞ **LINCOLN'S FATHER—THOMAS LINCOLN**

Thomas Lincoln was born January 1778 in Rockingham County, Virginia, the fourth child of Abraham and Bathsheba Lincoln. In 1782, the family moved to Kentucky, where they owned 1,200 acres of land.

Tragedy entered Thomas Lincoln's life in 1786, when he witnessed his father's death, massacred by Indians near Louisville, Kentucky. In the fall of 1786 he moved with his family to Washington County, Kentucky, where he was to live until he was eighteen years old.

From 1795 through 1802 Thomas worked at various jobs, acquiring skills as a farmer and carpenter. From 1802 to 1816 he lived in Har-

din County, Kentucky, where he purchased three farms totaling more than 816 acres and two Elizabethtown city lots.

On June 12, 1806, Thomas Lincoln married Nancy Hanks. The Lincolns had three children. While he lived in Hardin County, Thomas Lincoln was recorded as being a property appraiser, a road surveyor, and a jury member. Besides such civic responsibilities, he was involved in the activities of the Little Mount Separate Baptist Church, an antislavery congregation perhaps influential on Abraham Lincoln's later beliefs.

In December 1816 Thomas Lincoln and his

family left Kentucky for Indiana, where they settled in Little Pigeon Creek.

Nancy Hanks Lincoln died there of milk sickness two years later, and in 1819 Thomas married Sarah Bush Johnston, a widow. His new marriage brought three additional children — Elizabeth, Matilda, and John D. — into the Lincoln household. The children kept the Johnston name.

Thomas Lincoln assisted in the building of the Little Pigeon Creek Baptist Church in 1820. He served as a church trustee and as a member of the church conference. By 1824 he had cleared enough land on his Indiana farm to have ten acres of corn, five acres of wheat, and two acres of oats in addition to a large vegetable garden.

In 1830 the Lincoln family moved again — this time to Illinois. The promise of a better life there and fear of a new outbreak of milk sickness led Thomas Lincoln to his decision. Before he left he sold 80 acres of his Indiana farm for $125 and traded 20 acres for a horse. A lot in Elizabethtown, Kentucky belonging to Sarah Bush Lincoln was sold for $123. The fact that Thomas Lincoln also had 100 hogs and over 400 bushels of corn to sell suggests a sizable Indiana farm operation.

Thomas Lincoln purchased 40 acres of farmland in Coles County, Illinois (near present Charleston) in 1831. He sold this property in 1834 and purchased a larger farm of 200 acres in the Goose Nest Prairie area of Coles County. In 1837 he sold 120 acres of this farm for a profit of $87.50. This transaction left him free of debt and with 80 acres of good land.

Thomas Lincoln died at the age of 75 on January 17, 1851.

This letter, written on Christmas Eve and the only known one addressed to Thomas Lincoln from his son, suggests that their relationship was not close.

☞ LINCOLN'S MOTHER—NANCY HANKS

The mother of the sixteenth president was a person of mystery. Tradition and oral history trace her youthful life to Campbell County, Virginia as the daughter of Abraham and Sarah Harper Hanks. Orphaned at the age of nine, she is believed to have lived with relatives in North Carolina. Later, she moved to Kentucky with the family of a Richard Berry. It was in this household that she lived until her marriage.

Nancy Hanks married Thomas Lincoln, a carpenter, cabinetmaker, and farmer on June 12, 1806. Three children were born to them in the next five years—Sarah (born February 10, 1807), Abraham (born February 12, 1809), and Thomas, Jr. (born in 1811). Thomas, Jr. lived less than two years, and was buried near Knob Creek under a small triangular stone marked *T.L.*

Nancy Hanks Lincoln gathered the family household items and helped the family move over crude roads from Kentucky to Indiana in 1816. They settled in the northern part of the present Spencer County.

Life in the wilderness area of southern Indiana in the early nineteenth century exposed all of the family to hardships. A woman was

The Plant That Killed Lincoln's Mother

The white snakeroot plant *(Eupatorium rugosum)* responsible for Nancy Hanks Lincoln's death.

Milk sickness is an acute disease caused by eating dairy products or meat contaminated by a poisonous plant called white snakeroot *(Eupatorium rugosum)*. It is a shade-loving plant found throughout Indiana and commonly grows on roadsides and the north side of ridges and in damp open areas. The plant is also found in great quantities in most of the western half of Ohio and wooded parts of Illinois. In late summer, when the plant is in full bloom and has grown as high as four feet, its flat-topped clusters of small white flowers are easily recognized.

The sickness has been called puking fever, sick stomach, the slows, and the trembles. On the frontier it was most common in dry years, when cows wandered from poor pastureland to woods in search of food. There are records of many cases of milk sickness occurring in the winter and early summer, but the greatest incidence was in late summer and early fall. The symptoms are loss of appetite, listlessness, severe constipation, bad breath, and coma. Recovery is slow and may never be complete. Often an attack is fatal—as it was for Nancy Hanks Lincoln when milk sickness struck the Little Pigeon Creek settlement in the fall of 1818.

Although little was known about milk sickness until the twentieth century, its ravages were considerable. In Dubois County, Indiana, more than half of the deaths that occurred in the 1840s were attributed to it. The incidence of the disease tapered off as woodlands were cleared and cattle had better pasturage in dry weather. Today, the mixing of milk from several sources and pasteurization further reduce the likelihood of milk sickness.

expected to run the household, mend and sew, and provide comfort for husband and children.

Abraham Lincoln later wrote, "All that I am or ever shall hope to be I owe to my loving angel mother, God bless her."

Nancy Hanks Lincoln, who died on October 5, 1818, was buried in a whipsawed coffin held together by pegs young Abraham had whittled. She was laid to rest on a small knoll overlooking the family farm.

☞ LINCOLN'S SISTER—SARAH LINCOLN

Sarah Lincoln was born to Thomas and Nancy Hanks Lincoln in Elizabethtown, Kentucky on February 10, 1807. After her mother's death in 1818, she took care of the Lincoln household — cooking, cleaning, keeping the clothing in order, and looking after her father, brother, and cousin Dennis Hanks.

When Thomas Lincoln brought his new wife, Sarah Bush Johnston, and her three children to the Lincoln cabin in December 1819, Sarah Lincoln gained two new playmates — Elizabeth (Sarah's age) and Matilda (four years younger). Her stepmother described Sarah as short and somewhat plump with dark brown hair and grey eyes. Sarah's cousin John Hanks remembered her as kind, tender, good-natured, and smart. He also said her facial characteristics were somewhat similar to Abraham's. She was a modest, plain, industrious girl. Her face had a somber appearance which is believed to have been inherited from her mother.

On April 8, 1826, Sarah joined the Little Pigeon Creek Baptist Church. That same year, on August 2, she married Aaron Grigsby, and together they took up farming near their parents' homes. On January 20, 1828, Sarah and an infant died during childbirth. Both she and the child were buried in the Baptist Church Cemetery (now part of Lincoln State Park), Lincoln City, Indiana with a small sandstone marker bearing her initials above the grave. A larger marker was installed on May 30, 1916. Her husband is buried beside her.

☞ LINCOLN'S BROTHER—THOMAS LINCOLN, JR.

Thomas Lincoln, Jr.'s exact birth and death dates are unknown but it is generally believed he lived less than three years between 1811 and 1815. Poor recordkeeping and his short lifespan are probable reasons for the missing facts. The best available information indicates that he was born on the Knob Creek farm (about which Abraham Lincoln had his earliest memories) as the third child and the second son of Thomas and Nancy Hanks Lincoln. Thomas Lincoln, Jr. is buried in the Redmond family cemetery not far from the Knob Creek farm. The small triangular stone that originally marked the site has been removed, but a new marker was placed on the grave by the Boy Scouts of Des Moines, Iowa in September 1962.

This engraving of
Lincoln's stepmother,
Sarah Bush Johnston, is based on the
only surviving photograph of her taken
about 1865.

☞ LINCOLN'S STEPMOTHER—SARAH BUSH JOHNSTON

Sarah Bush Johnston Lincoln was born near Elizabethtown, Kentucky on December 13, 1788,
the youngest daughter of Christopher Bush in a
family of six boys and three girls. It is likely that
she met Thomas Lincoln in 1797, when he was
living and working in Elizabethtown. Sarah was
then nine years old and Thomas Lincoln was
twenty-one. Later, she came to know him better
as a guest at the Bush household on several
occasions. (Thomas Lincoln was working as a
patroller for Christopher Bush as early as 1806.)
There is a traditional story that in her youth
Sarah spurned Thomas Lincoln's advances and
rejected him for another suitor.

Sarah married Daniel Johnston on March 13,
1806. The Hardin County records show no property in Johnston's name and reveal that he was

once placed on the delinquent list for not paying
a poll tax. His wife's brothers sued him to
recover money he had borrowed from them. In
1814 Johnston was appointed jailer of the
county, but six men had to sign for his bond
instead of the usual two and none of his
brothers-in-law appeared as bondsmen. Subsequently, the Johnstons lived in a room above
the stone jail, and their youngest child, John D.,
was born there. Two daughters, Elizabeth and
Matilda, were born elsewhere in Elizabethtown.

The exact date of Daniel Johnston's death is
not known but the approximate time was the
summer of 1816. Using money from her father's
estate, Sarah purchased a cabin on property just
outside the city limits and moved there with her
three children. She had been a widow three

years when Thomas Lincoln returned from Kentucky and either began or renewed his courtship. They married on December 2, 1819.

Sarah made immediate preparations for the long journey to Kentucky. Her new family comprised the two Lincoln children, Sarah and Abraham; the Johnston children, Elizabeth, Matilda, and John D.; and an orphan named Dennis Hanks, whose foster parents had died at the same time as Nancy Hanks Lincoln. The new Mrs. Lincoln was thirty-one years old; her husband forty-two.

Abraham was ten years old when his father remarried. Until he was twenty-one he was under his stepmother's direction. One of the statements credited to her confirms the belief that she was an important factor in his education: "I induced my husband to permit Abe to read and study at home as well as at school. At first he was not easily reconciled to it but finally he too seemed willing to encourage him to a certain extent. . . . We took particular care not to disturb him—would let him read on and on until he quit of his own accord."

Dennis Hanks (beardless), the orphan who became a member of Sarah Bush Johnston's family when she married Thomas Lincoln in 1819, posed outside a reconstruction of the family's first Illinois log cabin that was exhibited in Chicago in 1865.

Lincoln's Schooling

In his homemade arithmetic book, a young Lincoln wrote "Abraham Lincoln/his hand and pen/he will be good but/god knows When."

During Abraham Lincoln's childhood schools on the frontier were often informal groups meeting infrequently. Classroom age varied widely. Instructors were often not much older than students. Textbooks and materials were scarce, and the schedule was likely to be interrupted whenever students were needed to work at home.

"... no qualification was ever required of a teacher beyond 'readin', writin', and cipherin' to the rule of three,'" Lincoln later wrote of frontier schooling. "If a straggler supposed to understand Latin happened to sojourn in the neighborhood, he was looked upon as a wizard. There was absolutely nothing to excite ambition for education. Of course, when I came of age I did not know much.... I could read, write, and cipher to the rule of three, but that was all. I have not been to school since. The little advance I now have upon this store of education, I have picked up from time to time under the pressure of necessity."

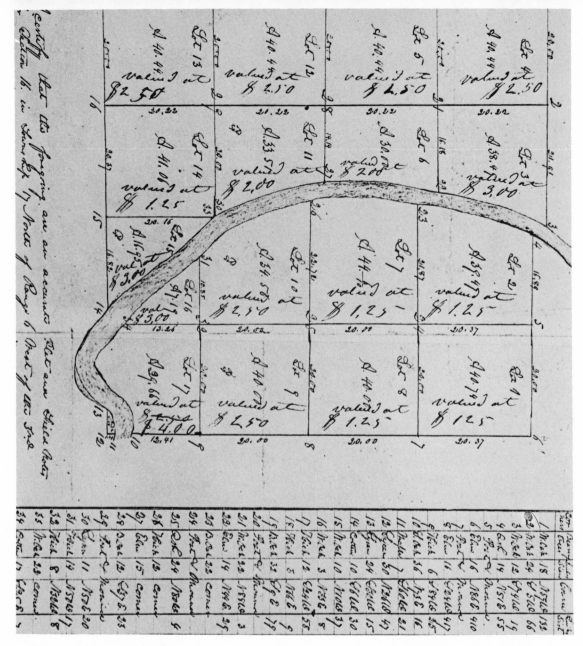

In this surveyor's map drawn for the Sangamon County Court, Lincoln designated property sizes, boundaries, and positions.

Lincoln the Surveyor

Lincoln, who may have learned to survey from his father, earned money surveying parts of Sangamon County, Illinois during the time he served in the state legislature. Measuring land to determine property boundaries was an important activity in a growing nation. George Washington worked as a surveyor in his youth and so did Thomas Jefferson. Lincoln's skill as a surveyor helped later when he plotted, or planned, a town in central Illinois that came to be named after him. Lincoln, Illinois is now the seat of Logan County.

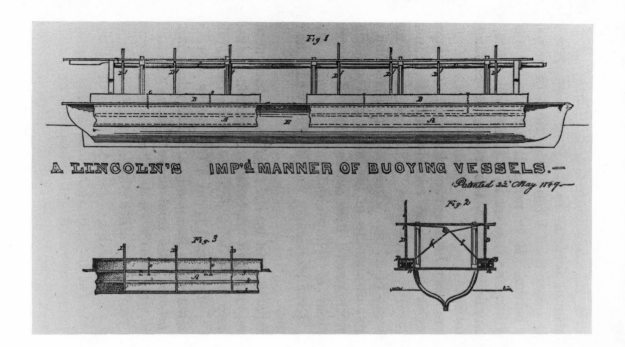

Lincoln the Riverman

Lincoln earned his first dollar as a young man in 1827 by ferrying passengers across the mouth of Anderson Creek in Indiana to steamers on the Ohio River. Waterways and transportation on them figured significantly in Lincoln's life. In 1828, with two friends he journeyed down the Mississippi River to New Orleans on a flatboat. Lincoln repeated the journey in 1831 with his stepbrother.

In 1848, Congressman Lincoln traveled on the Detroit River between Lake Erie and Lake Huron after a speaking tour of New England, and he may have seen a ship grounded on the shallow part of the river bed. When he reached Springfield, he had a model built of a device that would lift boats over such shoals by means of inflatable chambers made of rubberized cloth installed alongside the hull. The model (now in the Smithsonian Institution) accompanied a patent application that Lincoln filed in Washington the following year.

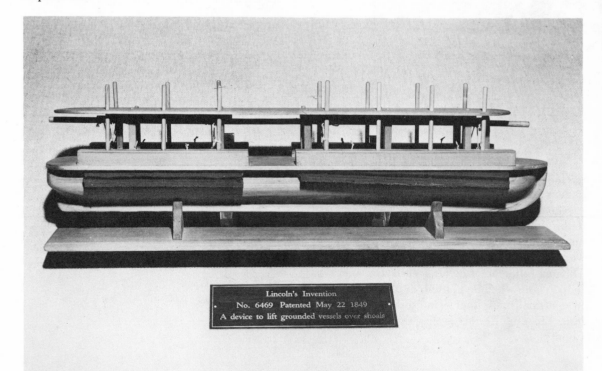

Lincoln's Invention
No. 6469 Patented May 22 1849
A device to lift grounded vessels over shoals

Lincoln the Suitor

Both of the two known romantic interests in Lincoln's life were named Mary and both came from Kentucky. Lincoln met Mary Owens in Springfield and proposed marriage to her in 1837. She turned him down. Later, when she was asked why, she said: "Mr. Lincoln was deficient in those little things which make up the chain of a woman's happiness—at least it was so in my case." A letter that Lincoln sent to a friend, Mrs. O. H. Browning, in 1838 offers a revealing look at his attitudes concerning courtship and marriage.

...in the autumn of 1836, a married lady of my acquaintance, and who was a great friend of mine, being about to pay a visit to her father and other relatives residing in Kentucky, proposed to me, that on her return she would bring a sister of hers with her, upon condition that I would engage to become her brother-in-law....I had seen the said sister some three years before, thought her intelligent and agreeable, and saw no good objection to plodding life through hand in hand with her—Time passed on, the lady took her journey and in due time returned, sister in company sure enough—This stomached me a little; for it appeared to me, that her coming so readily showed that she was a trifle too willing; but on reflection it occurred to me, that she might have been prevailed on by her married sister to come, without any thing concerning me ever having been mentioned to her; and so I concluded that if no other objection presented itself, I would consent to waive this....

In a few days we had an interview, and although I had seen her before, she did not look as my imagination had pictured her. I knew she was over-size, but she now appeared a fair match for Falstaff; I knew she was called an 'old maid' and I felt no doubt of the truth of at least half of the appelation; but now, when I beheld her, I could not for my life avoid thinking of my mother; and this, not from withered features, for her skin was too full of fat, to permit its contracting into wrinkles; but from her want of teeth, weather-beaten appearance in general, and from a kind of notion that ran in my head, that nothing could have commenced at the size of infancy, and reached her present bulk in less than thirtyfive or forty years; and, in short, I was not all pleased with

COTILLION PARTY.

E PLURIBUS UNUM.

The pleasure of your Company is respectfully solicited at a Cotillion Party, to be given at the "American House," on to-morrow evening at 7 o'clock, P. M.

December 16th, 1839.

N. H. RIDGELY,	J. F. SPEED,
J. A. M'CLERNAND,	J. SHIELDS,
R. ALLEN,	E. D. TAYLOR,
M. H. WASH,	E. H. MERRYMAN,
F. W. TODD,	N. E. WHITESIDE,
S. A. DOUGLASS,	M. EASTHAM,
W. S. PRENTICE,	J. R. DILLER,
N. W. EDWARDS,	A. LINCOLN,
	Managers.

In mid-nineteenth century Springfield, young men met young women at formally organized entertainments. Lincoln is the last-named sponsor of this 1839 party. Among the others are Stephen Douglas (Douglass), who was subsequently his political opponent, and Ninian Edwards, at whose house Lincoln was to meet his future wife.

her. But what could I do? I had told her sister that I would take her for better or for worse; and I made a point of honor and conscience in all things, to stick to my word....I determined to consider her my wife; and this done, all my powers of discovery were put to the rack, in search of perfections in her, which might be fairly set off against defects. I tried to imagine she was handsome, which, but for her unfortunate corpulency, was actually true—Exclusive of this, no woman that I have seen, has a finer face—I also tried to convince myself, that the mind was much more to be valued than the person; and in this, she was not inferior, as I could discover, to any with whom I had been acquainted....I now spent my time between planning how I might get along through life after my contemplated change of circumstances should have taken place; and I might procrastinate the evil day for a time....

19

After I had delayed the matter as long as I thought I could in honor do . . . I concluded I might as well bring it to a consummation without further delay; and so I mustered my resolution, and made the proposal to her direct; but, shocking to relate, she answered, No—At first I supposed she did it through an affectation of modesty, which I thought but ill-became her, under the peculiar circumstances of her case; but on my renewal of the charge, I found she repeled it with greater firmness than before—I tried again and again, but with the same success, or rather with the same want to success. I finally was forced to give it up, at which I very unexpectedly found myself mortified almost beyond endurance—I was mortified, it seemed to me, in a hundred different ways. My vanity was deeply wounded by the reflection, that I had so long been too stupid to discover her intentions, and at the same time never doubting that I understood them perfectly; and also, that she whom I had taught myself to believe nobody else would have, had actually rejected me with all my fancied greatness; and to cap the whole, I think, for the first time, began to suspect that I was really a little in love with her. But let it all go—I'll try and outlive it—Others have been made fools of by the girls; but this can never be with truth said of me—I most emphatically, in this instance, made a fool of myself—I have now come to the conclusion never again to think of marrying. . . .

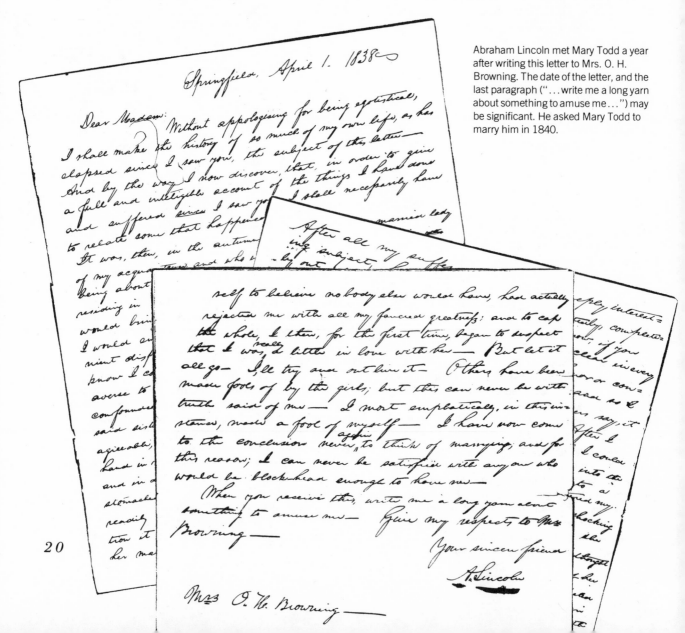

Abraham Lincoln met Mary Todd a year after writing this letter to Mrs. O. H. Browning. The date of the letter, and the last paragraph (". . . write me a long yarn about something to amuse me . . .") may be significant. He asked Mary Todd to marry him in 1840.

20

Lincoln's Marriage

Thirty-year-old Abraham Lincoln—tall, raw-boned, and skinny—met twenty-one-year-old Mary Todd in summer of 1839, when she was living with her sister, who was the daughter-in-law of the governor of Illinois. Social disparity as well as a twelve-inch difference in height may have prompted Lincoln to remark that they were "the long and the short of it." Mary Todd's parents were Eliza Ann Parker and Robert S. Todd. Her father was a grocer, banker, lawyer, cotton manufacturer, and clerk of the Kentucky House of Representatives. He married twice and raised thirteen children. Mary, born December 13, 1818 was the third daughter of his first wife.

The romance had its uneven moments and an engagement was temporarily broken off in 1841, but Lincoln and Mary Todd were married the following year. "Nothing new here," Lincoln noted at the end of a business letter written a week after the wedding, "except my marrying, which to me is a matter of profound wonder." The lawyer and his bride first moved into rooms in a tavern, but by 1844 had their own house in Springfield on the corner of Eighth and Jackson Streets.

Marriage certificate of Abraham Lincoln and Mary Todd. The license, which is dated 4 November 1842, was "solemnized" the same day. Rev. Charles Dresser, who signed the document as the officiating Episcopal minister, later sold the Lincolns his house at Eighth and Jackson Streets for $1,500.

THE PEOPLE OF THE STATE OF ILLINOIS.

To any Minister of the Gospel, or other authorised Person---GREETING.

THESE are to License and permit you to join in the holy bands of Matrimony *Abraham Lincoln* and *Mary Todd* of the County of Sangamon and State of Illinois, and for so doing, this shall be your sufficient warrant.

Given under my hand and seal of office, at Springfield, in said County this 4 day of *November* 1842

N. W. Matheny -Clerk.

Solemnized on the same 4th day of Nov. 1842   *Charles Dresser*

The earliest-known picture of Lincoln is a daguerreotype dating from four years after his marriage. This later photographic copy shows him as a very youthful-looking man of thirty-seven. Photography as we now know it is based on the work of several Europeans working independently in the early 1800s. The American inventor Samuel F. B. Morse played an important role in its introduction to this country in 1839—the year Lincoln met Mary Todd. This daguerreotype (named after its French inventor, Louis Jacques Mandé Daguerre) was made directly on a silver-coated copper plate. There was no negative and no possibility of multiple positive prints. Because the sitter had to stay still for several minutes before the picture-taking was complete, iron braces were often used to hold the head and back perfectly motionless. Such braces might explain Lincoln's stiff posture seen here.

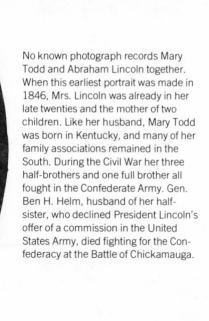

No known photograph records Mary Todd and Abraham Lincoln together. When this earliest portrait was made in 1846, Mrs. Lincoln was already in her late twenties and the mother of two children. Like her husband, Mary Todd was born in Kentucky, and many of her family associations remained in the South. During the Civil War her three half-brothers and one full brother all fought in the Confederate Army. Gen. Ben H. Helm, husband of her half-sister, who declined President Lincoln's offer of a commission in the United States Army, died fighting for the Confederacy at the Battle of Chickamauga.

The sitting room in the Springfield house as it appeared in the issue of *Frank Les-* *lie's Illustrated News* that followed Lincoln's inauguration.

The Springfield House

Immediately after Rev. Charles Dresser sold the Lincolns his five-year-old, one-story house for $1,500, the prosperous family added a second story. Between 1844 and 1860, when he was elected to the presidency, Lincoln amply supported his family as a lawyer, political speaker, and U.S. congressional representative. Their children lived in this house, and all but the eldest, Robert ("Rob"), were born in it.

This view was taken in 1860, shortly after Lincoln won the presidential nomination. Lincoln's tall, white-suited form can be seen at the right of the doorway.

Nameplate identifying the Springfield house appears above.

Lincoln the Poet

Young Lincoln penned doggerel rhymes like "Abraham Lincoln is my name/ And with my pen I write the same/ I work in both haste and speed/ and left it here for fools to read." Later, he attempted more ambitious poetry—"My Childhood Home I See Again" in 1844, followed by "Matthew Gentry," and "The Bear Hunt" in 1846.

While campaigning for Henry Clay in Indiana in 1844, he returned to the area where his mother and sister were buried and which he had left fifteen years earlier. "That part of the country..." he later wrote, "is as unpoetical as any spot on earth; but still, seeing it... aroused in me feelings which were certainly poetry." He wrote the following to express those feelings.

"My childhood's home I see again"

My childhood's home I see again,
 And sadden with the view;
And still, as memory crowds my brain,
 There's pleasure in it too.

O Memory! thou midway world
 'Twixt earth and paradise,
Where things decayed and loved ones lost
 In dreamy shadows rise,

And, freed from all that's earthly vile,
 Seem hallowed, pure, and bright,
Like scenes in some enchanted isle
 All bathed in liquid light.

As dusky mountains please the eye
 When twilight chases day;
As bugle-notes that, passing by
 In distance die away;

As leaving some grand waterfall
 We, lingering, list its roar—
So memory will hallow all
 We've known, but know no more.

Near twenty years have passed away
 Since here I bid farewell,
To woods and field, and scenes of play,
 And playmates loved so well.

Where many were, but few remain,
 Of old familiar things;
But seeing them, to mind again,
 The lost and absent brings.

The friends I left that parting day
 How changed, as time has sped!
Young childhood grown, strong manhood gray
 And half of all are dead.

I hear the loved survivors tell,
 How nought from death could save;
Till every sound appears a knell,
 And every spot a grave.

I range the fields with pensive tread,
 And pace the hollow rooms,
And feel (companion of the dead)
 I'm living in the tombs.

Matthew Gentry

But here's an object more of dread
 Than ought the grave contains—
A human form with reason fled,
 While wretched life remains.

Poor Matthew! Once of genius bright,
 A fortune-favored child—
Now locked for aye, in mental night,
 A haggard mad-man wild.

Poor Matthew! I have ne'er forgot
 When first, when maddened will,
Yourself you maimed, your father fought,
 And mother strove to kill;

When terror spread, and neighbours ran,
 Your dang'rous strength to bind;
And soon, a howling crazy man
 Your limbs were fast confined.

How then you strove and shrieked aloud,
 Your bones and sinews bared;
And fiendish on the gazing crowd,
 With burning eye-balls glared—

And begged, and swore, and wept and prayed,
 With maniac laugh[ter] joined—
How fearful were those signs displayed
 By pangs that killed thy mind!

And when at length, tho' drear and long,
 Time soothed thy fiercer woes,
How plaintively thy mournful song
 Upon the still night rose.

I've heard it oft, as if I dreamed,
    Far distant, sweet, and lone—
The funeral dirge, it ever seemed
    Of reason dead and gone.

To drink it's strains, I've stole away,
    All stealthily and still,
Ere yet the rising God of day
    Had streaked the Eastern hill.

Air held his breath; trees, with the spell,
    Seemed sorrowing angels round,
Whose swelling tears in dew-drops fell
    Upon the listening ground.

But this is past; and nought remains,
    That raised thee o'er the brute.
They piercing shrieks, and soothing strains,
    Are like, forever mute.

Now fare thee well—more thou the *cause*,
    Than *subject* now of woe.
All mental pangs, by time's kind laws,
    Hast lost the power to know.

O death! Thou awe-inspiring prince,
    That keepst the world in fear;
Why dost thou tear more blest ones hence,
    And leave him ling'ring here?

The Bear Hunt

A wild-bear chace, didst never see?
    Then hast thou lived in vain.
Thy richest bump of glorious glee,
    Lies desert in thy brain.

When first my father settled here,
    'Twas then the frontier line.
The panther's scream, filled night with fear
    And bears preyed on the swine.

But wo for Bruin's short lived fun,
    When rose the squealing cry;
How man and horse, with dog and gun,
    For vengeance, at him fly.

A sound of danger strikes his ear;
    He gives the breeze a snuff;
Away he bounds, with little fear,
    And seeks the tangled *rough*.

On press his foes, and reach the ground,
    Where's left his half munched meal;

The dogs, in circles, scent around,
    And find his fresh made trail.

With instant cry, away they dash,
    And men as fast pursue;
O'er logs they leap, through water splash,
    And shout the brisk halloo.

Now to elude the eager pack,
    Bear shuns the open ground;
Th[r]ough matted vines, he shapes his track
    An runs it, round and round.

The tall fleet cur, with deep-mouthed voice,
    Now speeds him, as the wind;
While half-grown pup, and short-legged fice,
    Are yelping far behind.

And fresh recruits are droppin in
    To join the merry *corps*;
With yelp and yell,—a mingled din—
    The woods are in a roar.

And round, and round the chace now goes,
    The world's alive with fun;
Nick Carter's horse, his rider throws,
    And more, Hill drops his gun.

Now sorely pressed, bear glances back,
    And lolls his tired tongue;
When as, to force him from his track,
    An ambush on him sprung.

Across the glade he sweeps for flight,
    And fully is in view.
The dogs, new-fired, by the sight,
    Their cry, and speed, renew.

The foremost ones, now reach his rear,
    He turns, they dash away;
And circling now the wrathful bear,
    They have him full at bay.

At top speed, the horse-men come,
    All screaming in a row.
"Whoop! Take him Tiger. Seize him Drum."
    Bang—bang—the rifles go.

And furious now, the dogs he tears,
    And crushes in his ire.
Wheels right and left, and upward rears,
    With eyes of burning fire.

But leaden death is at his heart.
    Vain all the strength he plies.
And, spouting blood from every part,
    He reels, and sinks and dies.

The top notice above (with several typo-
graphic errors) from the *Sangamo Jour-
nal* names Stephen Logan, who would
later become Lincoln's law partner; and
Edward Baker, Lincoln's friend and pre-
decessor as U.S. congressman, for
whom Lincoln's second son was named.
The middle notice announces Lincoln's
law partnership, and the bottom one
advertises the dissolution of Stuart's
previous partnership.

Lincoln the Lawyer

John T. Stuart, who befriended Lincoln during
their service in the Black Hawk War (1832), can
be credited with inspiring Lincoln's legal
career. A lawyer himself, he recognized Lincoln's interest in legal matters, and Lincoln read
and studied under his guidance. In 1836 Lincoln obtained his license as an attorney, and
with Stuart formed a partnership the following
year to practice law in Springfield. The firm was
dissolved in a friendly way in 1841. A second
partnership, with Stephen T. Logan, lasted for
three years. Lincoln's third and final partnership, with William H. Herndon, was formed in
1844. Because Illinois was divided into many
judicial units, or circuits, Lincoln had to travel
150 miles over nineteen counties to practice his
profession.

To the left is downtown Springfield, where Lincoln had his law office, as it looked in the 1850s. Streets were "paved" with split logs laid flat side up.

Lawyer Lincoln in a white Holland linen summer suit, 1858.

No known photograph shows Lincoln
and Douglas together, but because of
the enormous physical disparity (5'4" to
6'4"), Douglas, shown here in a daguerreotype, was nicknamed The Little
Giant. Lincoln's ultimate victory over
Douglas earned him the title of The
Giant Killer.

Lincoln the Legislator

Lincoln started his political career—which spanned thirty-five years and took him from the Illinois legislature to the White House—with a defeat, when he tried for a seat in the Illinois State Assembly in 1832. Although he won in his precinct, or voting district, he lost the election because the Whig party to which he belonged did not have a majority of votes throughout the state. The American Whig party was formed by men with objections to what they considered excessive power held by President Andrew Jackson. Lincoln remained a Whig until the organization of the Republican party in 1854—and six years later he became the nation's first Republican president.

Lincoln tried successfully for the Illinois State Assembly seat in 1834 and served four terms until 1841. In 1842 he declined an opportunity for reelection because his sights were set on a higher legislative post—a congressional seat in the U.S. House of Representatives. In Congress, he served from 1847 until 1849. He campaigned in 1846 for presidential candidate Zachary Taylor, hoping to be rewarded for his effort with the position of Commissioner of the General Land Office. Instead, he returned to his Springfield law practice at the end of his term in office and did not reenter politics until 1858, when he sought the U.S. Senate seat occupied by Democrat Stephen A. Douglas. Lincoln and Douglas debated their positions on issues including slavery in the summer and fall of 1858. Lincoln, who opposed introduction of slavery into the newly organized states of Kansas and Nebraska, lost the election to Douglas. The tables were turned two years later, when Lincoln and Douglas again competed—in the presidential race.

Lincoln's Autobiographies

Details about Lincoln's life, his conversations, opinions, and actions come from many sources, including the writings of his presidential secretaries, John Hay and John Nicolay. But it is Lincoln's own words that tell us most of what we know about the man before he was president.

Two autobiographies are known to exist. The first is three pages in Lincoln's hand, written in December 1859. A much longer version, which includes stories about Lincoln's youth on the frontier, was dated June 1860, after he had won the Republican presidential nomination.

The opening paragraph of Lincoln's shorter autobiography.

Lincoln sent his first, brief autobiography to Jesse W. Fell of Bloomington, Illinois with the following note: "Herewith is a little sketch, as you requested. There is not much of it, for the reason, I suppose, that there is not much of me. If anything is made out of it, I wish it to be modest and not to go beyond the material. If it were thought necessary to incorporate anything from any of my speeches, I suppose there would be no objection. Of course it must not appear to have been written by myself."

I was born February 12, 1809, in Hardin County, Kentucky. My parents were both born in Virginia, of undistinguished families —second families, perhaps I should say. My mother, who died in my tenth year, was of a family of the name Hanks, some of whom now reside in Adams, and others in Macon County, Illinois. My paternal grandfather, Abraham Lincoln, emigrated from Rockingham County, Virginia, to Kentucky about 1781 or 1782, where a year or two later he was killed by Indians: not in battle, but by stealth, when he was laboring to open a farm in the forest. His ancestors, who were Quakers, went to Virginia from Berks County, Pennsylvania. An effort to identify them with the New England family of the same name ended in nothing more definate than a similarity of Christian names in both families, such as Enoch, Levi, Mordecai, Solomon, Abraham, and the like.

My father, at the death of his father, was but six years of age, and he grew up literally without education. He removed from Kentucky to what is now Spencer County, Indiana, in my eighth year. We reached our new home about the time the State came into the Union. It was a wild region, with many bears and other wild animals still in the woods. There I grew up....

I was raised to farm work, which I continued till I was twenty-one. At twenty-one I came to Illinois, Macon County. Then I got to New Salem, at the time in Sangamon, now in Menard County, where I remained a year as a sort of clerk in a store. Then came the Black Hawk War; and I was elected a captain of volunteers, a success which gave me more pleasure than any I have had since. I went to the campaign, was elected, ran

An early advertisement for Lincoln's presidential candidacy is a typical piece of 1860 campaign literature.

for Legislature the same year (1832) and was beaten —the only time I have ever been beaten by the people. The next and three succeeding biennial elections I was elected to the Legislature. I was not a candidate afterward. During this legislative period I had studied law, and removed to Springfield to practice it. In 1846 I was once elected to the Lower House of Congress. Was not a candidate for reelection. From 1849 to 1854, both inclusive, practiced law more assiduously than ever before. Always a Whig in politics; and generally on the Whig electoral tickets, making active canvasses. I was losing interest in politics when the repeal in the Missouri Compromise aroused me again. What I have done since is pretty well known.

If any personal description of me is thought desirable, it may be said that I am, in height, six feet four inches, nearly; lean in flesh, weighing on the average one hundred and eighty pounds; dark complexion, with coarse black hair and grey eyes. No other marks or brands recollected.

31

The Presidential Candidate

This 1860 cartoon entitled "The Coming Man's Presidential Career, a la Blondin" raises questions about candidate Lincoln's abilities to successfully balance slavery with Constitutional issues. A misstep could send everything "To the whirlpool." Charles Blondin was a French tightrope walker. The whirlpool sign alludes to his crossing Niagara Falls in 1855, 1859, and 1860.

The ranks of the Democratic party were disastrously split between two candidates—Douglas and Breckinridge—in the 1860 presidential race. In this Currier and Ives lithograph, Lincoln is about to feast on Democratic opponents who are symbolically depicted on the half shell. Breckinridge's complaint about being eaten "by a rail splitter" reflects the many public jibes at Lincoln's rural background.

The lower left lithograph suggests that Douglas must deal with the issue of slavery if he wants to cross the Lincoln-built rail fence and succeed in the presidential race. The lithograph clearly favors the long-legged Lincoln.

As the presidential election of 1860 took shape, Lincoln's opposition to slavery made him a popular political figure in northern cities. Early in the year the Chicago press endorsed him for president and, shortly after, when he addressed a New York City audience of fifteen hundred at Cooper Institute, the New York *Tribune* called him "the greatest man since St. Paul." At the Republican convention in Chicago in May 1860, Lincoln received the presidential nomination on the third ballot. (Little more than a year earlier, however, Lincoln expressed doubts about seeking political office when he said in a letter, "I do not think myself fit for the Presidency.") The opposition was split three ways: the northern Democrats nominated Stephen Douglas; the southern Democrats nominated John C. Breckinridge; and John Bell was the nominee of the Constitutional Union Party.

Lincoln the presidential candidate before growing his beard (1860).

Lincoln's Beard

Like much of his correspondence, Lincoln's reply to Grace Bedell was written by himself. Although he thought whiskers might be considered a "silly affection" in the fall of 1860, he had reversed his opinion by the following spring.

Private

Springfield, Ill. Oct 19. 1860

Miss Grace Bedell

My dear little Miss.

Your very agreeable letter of the 15th is received—

I regret the necessity of saying I have no daughter— I have three sons— one seventeen, one nine, and one seven, years of age— They, with their mother, constitute my whole family—

As to the whiskers, having never worn any, do you not think people would call it a piece of silly affection if I were to begin it now?

Your very sincere well-wisher

A. Lincoln.

Lincoln was the first bearded president of the United States. Eleven-year-old Grace Bedell of Westfield, New York may have affected his decision to grow a beard when she wrote him in 1860 that ". . . you would look a great deal better for your face is so thin. All the ladies like whiskers and they would tease their husbands to vote for you." (Women could not cast their own votes until 1920, when the Nineteenth Constitutional Amendment was passed.) At first Lincoln rejected the idea but by March 1861, when he reached Washington, D.C. for his inauguration, he had a beard.

This photograph, taken on November 25, 1860, a little more than a month after Lincoln replied to Grace Bedell, shows the beginning of a beard.

BELLINGHAM'S STIMULATING ONGUENT FOR THE HAIR & WHISKERS

PRESIDENT LINCOLN.
PRESIDENT LINCOLN.
PRESIDENT LINCOLN.

DID YOU SEE HIM?

DID YOU SEE HIS MUSTACHE?
DID YOU SEE HIS MUSTACHE?
DID YOU SEE HIS MUSTACHE?

DID YOU SEE HIS WHISKERS?
DID YOU SEE HIS WHISKERS?
DID YOU SEE HIS WHISKERS?

RAISED IN SIX WEEKS BY THE USE OF

BELLINGHAM'S ONGUENT.

SEND FOR A BOX BY RETURN MAIL. PRICE

One Dollar a Box.

HORACE L. HEGEMAN & CO.,

DRUGGISTS, &C.,

24 William Street, New York

DO YOU WANT WHISKERS?

DO YOU WANT A MUSTACHE?

BELLINGHAM'S

CELEBRATED

STIMULATING ONGUENT,

For the Whiskers and Hair.

The subscribers take pleasure in announcing to the citizens of the United States, that they have obtained the agency for, and are now enabled to offer to the American public, the above justly celebrated and world renowned article.

THE STIMULATING ONGUENT

is prepared by DR. C. P. BELLINGHAM, an eminent physician of London, and is warranted to bring out a thick set of

WHISKERS OR A MUSTACHE,

in from three to six weeks. This article is the only one of the kind used by the French, and in London and Paris it is in universal use.

It is a beautiful, economical, soothing, yet stimulating compound, acting as if by magic upon the roots, causing a beautiful growth of luxuriant hair. If applied to the scalp, it will cure BALDNESS, and cause to spring up in place of the bald spots a fine growth of new hair. Applied according to directions, it will turn RED or towy hair DARK, and restore gray hair to its original color, leaving it soft, smooth, and desirable. The "ONGUENT" is an indispensable article in every gentleman's toilet, and after one week's use they would not for any consideration be without it.

One of the first photographs of the six-teenth president with his new beard (1861)

An 1861 advertisement (left) suggests Lincoln had a moustache as well as a beard, but no known photographs support this.

The President's new style gave rise to many cartoons in the popular press such as the one below from *Vanity Fair*.

3 5

The Inauguration

THE NEW PRESIDENT OF THE UNITED STATES
FROM A FUGITIVE SKETCH.

Lincoln was sworn into office as President of the United States in March 1861—one month after Jefferson Davis was elected to lead the Confederate states. South Carolina, which seceded from the Union after Lincoln's election, was followed by Mississippi, Florida, Alabama, Georgia, Louisiana, and Texas by the time of his inauguration. They were joined in April by Arkansas, North Carolina, Virginia, and Tennessee to comprise the eleven-state Confederacy.

Lincoln was scheduled to make an address in Baltimore as he proceeded to Washington for his inauguration, but rumor of an assassination plot changed his plans and he traveled through the city early in the morning without speaking. One exaggerated newspaper account reported him wearing a Scotch cap and plaid suit as disguise. Numerous cartoons like the one above from *Vanity Fair* suggested that even a long military cape would be insufficient to keep his tall figure unidentified.

The photograph (on the left) of the 1861 inauguration before the Capitol's east portico shows the building still without its cast-iron dome.

On the right is the conclusion of the final draft of Lincoln's 1861 inaugural address with his handwritten corrections on the printer's galley.

improved, I make no recommendations of amendments. I am, rather, for the old ship, and the chart of the old pilots. If, however, the people desire a new, or an altered vessel, the matter is exclusively their own, and they can move in the premises, as well without as with an executive recommendation. I shall place no obstacle in the way of what may appear to be their wishes.

The Chief Magistrate derives all his authority from the people, and they have conferred none upon him to fix terms for the separation of the States. The people themselves can do this *also* if they choose; but the executive, as such, has nothing to do with it. His duty is to administer the present government, as it came to his hands, and to transmit it, unimpaired by him, to his successor.

Why should there not be a patient confidence in the ultimate justice of the people? Is there any better or equal hope, in the world? In our present differences, is either party without faith *of being* in the right? If the Almighty Ruler of nations, with his eternal truth and justice, be on *on your side of the North, or on yours of the South,* that truth, and that justice, will surely prevail, by the judgment of this great tribunal, the American people.

By the frame of the government under which we live, this same people have wisely given their public servants but little power for mischief; and have, with equal wisdom, provided for the return of that little to their own hands at very short intervals. While the people *retain their virtue, and vigilence, no administration* by any extreme of wickedness or folly, can very seriously injure the government in the short space of four years.

My countrymen, one and all, *think calmly and* well, upon this whole subject. Nothing valuable can be lost by taking time. If there be an object to *hurry* any of you, in hot haste, to a step which you would never take *deliberately*, that object will be frustrated by taking time; but no good object can be frustrated by it. Such of you as are now dissatisfied, still have the old Constitution unimpaired, and, on the sensitive point, the laws of your own framing under it; while the new administration will have no immediate power, if it would, to change either. If it were admitted that you who are dissatisfied, hold the right side in the dispute, there still is no single good reason for precipitate action. Intelligence, patriotism, Christianity, and a firm reliance on Him, who has never yet forsaken this favored land, are still competent to adjust, in the best way, all our present difficulty.

In *your* hands, my dissatisfied fellow countrymen, and not in *mine*, is the momentous issue of civil war. The government will not assail *you*. You can have no conflict, without being yourselves the aggressors. *You* have no oath registered in Heaven to destroy the government, while *I* shall have the most solemn one to "preserve, protect and defend" it.

☞ I am loth to close. We are not enemies, but friends— We must not be enemies. Though passion may have strained, it must not break our bonds of affection. The mystic chords of memory, streching from every battlefield, and patriot grave, to every living heart and hearthstone, all over this broad land, will yet swell the chorus of the Union, when again touched, as surely they will be, by the better angels of our nature.

The Executive Mansion

Although Abraham Lincoln himself referred to it as the White House, the Washington house that he and his family occupied was officially called the Executive Mansion during his administration. Earlier, it had a variety of names, formal and informal. A 1792 advertisement sought building proposals for a "President's House," and on a resulting set of architect's plans it was labeled "Palace." A Baltimore newspaper referred to it as the "white house" as early as 1810—probably because its light sandstone exterior contrasted with surrounding brick and frame buildings—but the name was not official until it appeared on presidential stationery in 1901. The large, four-story building was designed for many uses and contained offices for the president and his staff, as well as reception rooms for entertaining political and foreign dignitaries. The Lincoln family had private living quarters on an upstairs floor.

During the hot August of 1863, Mary Todd Lincoln and her children stayed at Anderson Cottage on the grounds of Soldiers' Home north of Washington. In a letter written on Executive Mansion stationery shortly after their departure from the city, the president calls their residence the White House.

> *Executive Mansion,*
>
> *Washington, August 8 1863.*
>
> *My dear Wife.*
>
> *All as well as usual, and no particular trouble any way. I put the money into the Treasury at five per cent, with the privilege of withdrawing it any time upon thirty day's notice. I suppose you are glad to learn this. Tell dear Tad, poor "Nanny Goat," is lost, and Mrs. Cuthbert & I are in distress about it. The day you left Nanny was found resting herself, and chewing her little cud, on the middle of Tad's bed. But now she's gone! The gardener kept complaining that she destroyed the flowers, till it was concluded to bring her down to the White House. This was done, and the second day, she had disappeared,*

Because Washington was close to the secessionist state of Virginia and many Washington residents were sympathetic to the Confederacy, special measures were taken to protect government buildings in the nation's capital after the beginning of the Civil War. This print shows Union soldiers garrisoned in the ornate East Room during Lincoln's presidency; but the same room, largest in the Executive Mansion, was the scene of many state receptions in the same era.

The drawing at left provides an exact record of the furnishing of the Cabinet Room in the Lincoln White House — including such fine details as the gas line leading from chandelier to table lamp. The gas line also appears in the engraving above showing Lincoln and his cabinet members meeting with Lieutenant-General Winfield Scott. Around the foreshortened table are (l. to r.) Edward Baker, attorney general; Gideon Welles, secretary of the navy; Montgomery Blair, postmaster general; William H. Seward, secretary of state; Salmon P. Chase, secretary of the treasury; Lincoln; Scott, general-in-chief of the army; Caleb B. Smith, secretary of the interior; and Simon Cameron, secretary of war. The base of the unfinished Washington Monument appears in the left window.

The President's Family

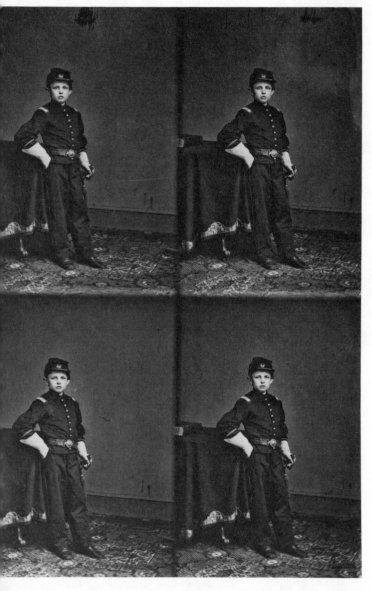

This undated photograph of Thomas ("Tad") Lincoln in Union uniform was made when his father, as president, was commander-in-chief of the army. The horizontal pairs of such "four-image" photographs could be used to compose three-dimensional pictures when viewed through a stereopticon.

Robert Todd Lincoln in 1865, shortly before his father's assassination.

Robert Todd Lincoln
(August 1, 1843-July 26, 1926)
"Rob" was named for his grandfather Robert Todd. As the only Lincoln child to reach maturity, he experienced the deaths of his brothers and his parents. Robert Lincoln married Mary Harlen and had three children: Mary, Abraham, and Jessie. He was a Harvard Law School graduate but later he turned to business and became president of the Pullman Company. He served as secretary of war under President Garfield and, later, as United States ambassador to Great Britain. Robert Lincoln died at his home in Vermont at the age of 83. He is buried at

William Wallace ("Willie") Lincoln was photographed by Mathew Brady several times between his father's inauguration in 1860 and his own early death in 1862.

Arlington National Cemetery in Washington, D.C., the only Lincoln son not interred in the Springfield, Illinois Oak Ridge Cemetery.

Edward Baker Lincoln
(March 10, 1846-February 1, 1850)

Edward was the second son born to Abraham and Mary Todd Lincoln. He was named for Edward Dickinson Baker, a friend and political associate of his father. The cause of his early death is unknown although diphtheria has been suggested. No photograph is known to exist of Edward Baker Lincoln. He is buried in the Lincoln Tomb in the Oak Ridge Cemetery at Springfield, Illinois.

William Wallace Lincoln
(December 21, 1850-February 20, 1862)

The third Lincoln son, "Willie," was named for William Wallace, Mary Todd Lincoln's brother-in-law. William was said to be the most lovable of the Lincoln children and a good student. He liked to ride his pony around the White House grounds. An ailment, which was fatal, was variously diagnosed as bilious fever, typhoid, and acute malarial infection. He is buried in the Lincoln Tomb in the Oak Ridge Cemetery at Springfield, Illinois.

Thomas Lincoln
(April 4, 1853-July 15, 1871)

"Tad," the fourth and youngest Lincoln son, had a speech impediment that caused him to lisp. With William he was responsible for many jokes and pranks in the White House. After the assassination of his father, Tad and his mother lived in Europe for three years. This is where he apparently contracted his fatal illness diagnosed as "pleurisy...probably tubercular in origin." He is buried in the Lincoln Tomb in the Oak Ridge Cemetery at Springfield, Illinois.

This engraving from an 1864 photograph by Mathew Brady showing eleven-year-old Thomas ("Tad") and the president is the only one known in which Abraham Lincoln wears glasses.

When Mary Todd Lincoln arrived in Washington as First Lady in 1861, her family consisted of Robert (age eighteen), William (age eleven), and Thomas (age eight). Much has been written about the lack of discipline she exercised over her children, but from her husband's remarks it appears that she did not spare the rod when she felt it could do some good.

Of the letters between Mary Todd Lincoln and her husband, many demonstrate the concerns of a mother raising children at home. In one letter she asks her husband to find some plaid stockings for "Eddy's dear little feet." Of the responsibilities and work involved with the children, she wrote: "I feel wearied and tired enough to know that this is Saturday night, our babies are asleep."

Mary Todd Lincoln was a mother in a time when at least 25 percent of infant mortality occurred within the first two and one-half years of life. Although she was spared that grief, the first in a series of family tragedies occurred when her youngest child, Edward, died at the age of four in 1850.

Mary Todd Lincoln had an interest in fashion that included elaborate floral headpieces and dresses with long trains. On seeing her in such a dress with yards of material trailing behind her, Lincoln once remarked, "Whew! Our cat has a long tail tonight." This photograph by Mathew Brady (above) shows Mrs. Lincoln in the gown she wore to the 1861 inaugural ball. Its full shape was obtained by a wire frame worn beneath the skirt.

Mrs. Lincoln was severely criticized by the public during her years as the president's wife. She was called a traitor by her southern friends and was admonished for spending federal money needed for the war effort to fix up the White House. It is generally accepted that with the death of a second child, William, in 1862 Mrs. Lincoln became mentally disturbed. The assassination of her husband in 1865 led to her collapse, and soon after she was placed in an asylum. When she was released, she returned to Springfield, Illinois, where she died in 1882.

The Civil War

Lincoln had been in office little more than a month when troops under the command of General P. G. T. Beauregard bombarded Fort Sumter in the harbor of Charleston, South Carolina in the name of the newly-formed Confederacy of eleven states (South Carolina, Mississippi, Florida, Alabama, Georgia, North Carolina, Texas, Arkansas, Louisiana, Tennessee, and Virginia) led by Jefferson Davis. The action marked the beginning of the Civil War that engulfed the nation for four years, destroyed its youth, and left the South a shambles. It is now seen as having involved complex social, economic, and political developments, but the issues that most concerned and inflamed the active participants were slavery and the rights of states to determine independent action. Peace was declared at Appomattox Courthouse, Virginia, on April 9, 1865, when Confederate General Robert E. Lee surrendered to Union General Ulysses S. Grant.

Inscribed to the 8th Wisconsin Reg!

"OLD ABE" THE BATTLE EAGLE

SONG & CHORUS
Poetry by
L. J. BATES ESQ.

MUSIC BY
T. MARTIN TOWNE
Author of 'Ourboys are coming home'

MILWAUKEE
Published by H.N. HEMPSTED 410 Main St.

The hero of this song, "Old Abe," was an eagle originally caught by the Chippewa Indian Chief Sky and later sold to a young Union recruit, Johnny Hill. Old Abe became the mascot of the Eighth Regiment, Wisconsin Volunteers, and he would fly high above the troops as they went into action, often jabbering raucously as if urging the men to action. After the war, Old Abe went on tours of the country and helped raise thousands of dollars for war relief charity.

Nowhere is Lincoln's height more apparent than in this Mathew Brady photograph made on the Antietam battlefield near Sharpsburg, Maryland in 1862.

Emancipation Proclamation

Lincoln as he appeared in 1865 during the last year of the Civil War. This "stereo card" was actually made of images taken by a multiple lens camera.

The Emancipation Proclamation (issued in preliminary form September 1862 and in final form for official signature January 1, 1863) ended slavery in the United States. It won European support for the Union cause and dissuaded Britain (where slavery ended in 1840) and France from supporting the Confederacy. Not all of Northern opinion was in favor of Lincoln's bold action, which was subject to widespread criticism in the press. "If I could save the Union without freeing any slave, I would do it; and if I could save it by freeing some and leaving others alone, I would also do that," Lincoln said in reply to Horace Greeley, newspaper editor and publisher of the New York *Tribune*. This section of the Emancipation Proclamation in Lincoln's handwriting shows his correction of "gradual *adoption* of slavery" to "gradual *abolishment* of slavery."

By the President of the
United States of America
A Proclamation

I Abraham Lincoln, President of the United States of America, and commander-in-chief of the Army and Navy thereof, do hereby proclaim and declare that hereafter, as heretofore, the war will be prosecuted for the object of practically restoring the constitutional relations between the United States, and each of the states, and the people thereof, in which states that relation is, or may be suspended, or disturbed.

of cong...
and to puni...
confiscate property of...
Approved July 17. 1862, and a...
joint Resolution explanatory thereof,
published, I, Abraham Lincoln, Presi-
the United States, do hereby proclaim to, and
warn all persons within the contemplation of
said sixth section to cease participating in, aiding, countenancing, or abetting the existing rebellion, or any rebellion against the government
of the United States, and to return to their proper allegiance to the United States, on pain of the
forfeitures and seizures, as within and by said
sixth section provided.

And I hereby make known that it is my
purpose, upon the next meeting of Congress, to again
recommend the adoption of a practical measure
for tendering pecuniary aid to the free choice or
rejection, of any and all States which may then
be recognizing and practically sustaining the authority of the United States, and which may then have
voluntarily adopted, or thereafter may voluntarily
adopt, gradual abolishment of slavery within
such State or States—that the object is to practically restore, thenceforward to be maintained, the constitutional relation between the general government,
and each, and all the states, wherein that relation

& participa...

ong countervailing

onclusive evidence that
... the people thereof, are not then
... rellion against the United States,

That attention is hereby called to an Act of Congress entitled An Act to make an additional
Article of War. Approved March 13. 1862, and
which act is in the words and figures following.

Be it enacted by the Senate and House of Representatives of the United
States of America in Congress assembled. That hereafter the following
shall be promulgated as an additional article of war for the government
of the army of the United States and shall be obeyed and observed as
such.

Article —. All officers or persons in the military or naval service of
the United States are prohibited from employing any of the forces under
their respective commands for the purpose of returning fugitives from service or labor, who may have escaped from any persons to whom such service or labor is claimed to be due, and any officer who shall be found
guilty by a court-martial of violating this article shall be dismissed from
the service.

Sec. 2. And be it further enacted. That this act shall take effect from
and after its passage.

Also to the. ninth. and tenth sections of an
Act entitled An Act to suppress Insurrection,
to punish Treason and Rebellion, to seize and confiscate property of rebels, and for other purposes,"
Approved July 17. 1862, and which sections are
in the words and figures following.

Sec. 9. And be it further enacted. That all slaves of persons who
shall hereafter be engaged in rebellion against the government of the
United States or who shall in any way give aid or comfort thereto, escap-
ing from such persons and taking ...

Address delivered at the dedication of the Cemetery at Gettysburg.

Four score and seven years ago our fathers brought forth on this continent, a new nation, conceived in Liberty, and dedicated to the proposition that all men are created equal.

Now we are engaged in a great civil war, testing whether that nation, or any nation so conceived and so dedicated, can long endure. We are met on a great battle field of that war. We have come to dedicate a portion of that field, as a final resting place for those who here gave their lives that that nation might live. It is altogether fitting and proper that we should do this.

But, in a larger sense, we can not dedicate — we can not consecrate — we can not hallow — this ground. The brave men, living and dead, who struggled here have consecrated it, far above our poor power to add or detract. The world will little note, nor long remember what we say here, but it can never forget what they did here. It is for us the living, rather, to be dedicated here to the unfinished work which they who fought here have thus far so nobly advanced. It is rather for us to be here dedicated to the great task remaining before us — that from these honored dead we take increased devotion to that cause for which they gave the last full measure of devotion — that we here highly resolve that these dead shall not have died in vain — that this nation, under God, shall have a new birth of freedom — and that government of the people, by the people, for the people, shall not perish from the earth.

Abraham Lincoln.

November 19, 1863.

Gettysburg Battlefield dedication.

On November 19, 1863 Lincoln participated in dedication ceremonies at Gettysburg, Pennsylvania to commemorate the battle between Union and Confederate troops in which some 48,000 soldiers were killed, wounded, or listed as missing. A Union victory, it marked the beginning of a decline in Confederate strength. The Harrisburg (Pennsylvania) *Press* commented on Lincoln's speech: "We pass over the silly remarks of the President; for the credit of the nation we are willing that the veil of oblivion shall be dropped

Lincoln's holograph, or handwritten, copy of the Gettysburg Address. There were six holograph copies of the Gettysburg Address and five are known to exist, all with slight differences. The first draft was written in Washington and Lincoln may have worked on his speech on the train from Washington to Pennsylvania. The version shown here varies in detail from the spoken address.

The Gettysburg Address

over them and that they shall no more be repeated or thought of." *The New York Times* printed the speech in full but the *New York Herald* printed only a small mention of the event near the financial section and noted simply that, "Dedicatory remarks of the President of the United States" were part of the program. Lincoln contracted a form of smallpox called varioloid at about the time of his speech and was bedridden for three weeks afterward.

Four score and seven years ago our fathers brought forth on this continent, a new nation, conceived in Liberty, and dedicated to the proposition that all men are created equal. Now we are engaged in a great civil war, testing whether that nation, or any nation so conceived or so dedicated, can long endure. We are met on a great battle field of that war. We have come to dedicate a portion of that field, as the final resting place for those who here gave their lives that that nation might live. It is altogether fitting and proper that we should do this. But, in a larger sense, we cannot dedicate—we cannot consecrate—we cannot hallow—this ground. The brave men, living and dead, who have struggled here, have consecrated it, far above our poor power to add or detract. The world will little note, nor long remember what we say here, but it can never forget what they did here. It is for us the living, rather, to be dedicated here to the unfinished work which they who fought here have thus far so nobly advanced. It is rather for us to be here dedicated to the great task remaining before us—that from these honored dead we take increased devotion to that cause for which they gave the last full measure of devotion—that we here highly resolve that these dead shall not have died in vain—that this nation, under God, shall have a new birth of freedom—and that government of the people, by the people, for the people, shall not perish from the earth.

THANKSGIVING — DAY.

THE UNION ALTAR.

In 1789 George Washington proclaimed a national holiday commemorating the Plymouth Colony harvest of 1621, but in ensuing years it was sporadically observed from one year to the next and not in all parts of the country. Lincoln was urged to recognize it again by Sarah J. Hale, feminist, editor of *Godey's Lady's Book* and author of the poem, "Mary Had a Little Lamb." In 1863, Lincoln revived the observation and stabilized celebration on the last Thursday of November.

This 1863 woodcut by Thomas Nast, a political cartoonist also known for his widely-reproduced depiction of a red-cheeked, white-bearded Santa Claus, is titled "Columbia at the Union Altar." Thanksgiving Day was especially significant for families with sons who survived service in the Civil War.

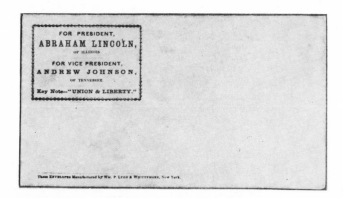

Commercial firms plainly advertised their contributions to the presidential campaign. This 1864 envelope with corner imprint came from a New York commercial stationer.

Reelection

The outlook for Lincoln's reelection did not appear promising at the start of 1864. The Union army, of which he was commander-in-chief, had made weak progress against the Confederates, and some Republicans believed his Emancipation Proclamation to be too lenient. Many voiced doubts of his ability to lead the country through a second four years and bring the Civil War to a peaceful close. Nevertheless, at the Republican Convention held in July 1864, Lincoln was unanimously nominated as the presidential candidate with Andrew Johnson replacing Hannibal Hamlin as his vice-presidential running mate.

Campaign posters and parade lantern from the 1864 election.

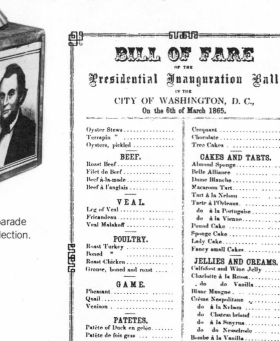

Menu from Lincoln's second inaugural ball.

Photograph of a smiling Lincoln was taken in Alexander Gardner's Washington studio five days before the president's death.

Shortly after ten o'clock on Friday evening, April 14, 1865, as Lincoln watched Laura Keene perform in *Our American Cousin* at Ford's Theatre a few blocks from the White House, a young actor named John Wilkes Booth opened the door to the presidential box. Sitting with the president were Mary Todd Lincoln and their guests Clara Harris and her fiance, Major Henry Reed Rathbone (the daughter and stepson of Senator Harris of New York). Some time before Booth entered the box, Lincoln had reached for his wife's hand. Mary Todd Lincoln whispered, "What will Miss Harris think?" and Lincoln responded, "She won't think anything about it." These were Abraham Lincoln's last words. Booth, who wanted to sustain the Confederacy despite Lee's surrender the preceding week, shot Lincoln through the neck with a small derringer, jumped to the stage, and disappeared. Mortally wounded, the president was carried to a lodging house across the street, where he died the next morning at 7:22 a.m.

Assassination

Reward poster issued immediately after the assassination with descriptions of Booth and two of his accomplices.

War Department, Washington, April 20, 1865.

$100,000 REWARD!

THE MURDERER

Of our late beloved President, ABRAHAM LINCOLN,

IS STILL AT LARGE.

$50,000 REWARD!

will be paid by this Department for his apprehension, in addition to any reward offered by Municipal Authorities or State Executives.

$25,000 REWARD!

will be paid for the apprehension of JOHN H. SURRATT, one of Booth's accomplices.

$25,000 REWARD!

will be paid for the apprehension of DANIEL C. HARROLD, another of Booth's accomplices.

LIBERAL REWARDS will be paid for any information that shall conduce to the arrest of either of the above-named criminals, or their accomplices.

All persons harboring or secreting the said persons, or either of them, or aiding or assisting their concealment or escape, will be treated as accomplices in the murder of the President and the attempted assassination of the Secretary of State, and shall be subject to trial before a Military Commission and the punishment of DEATH.

Let the stain of innocent blood be removed from the land by the arrest and punishment of the murderers.

All good citizens are exhorted to aid public justice on this occasion. Every man should consider his own conscience charged with this solemn duty, and rest neither night nor day until it be accomplished.

EDWIN M. STANTON, Secretary of War.

DESCRIPTION.—BOOTH is 5 feet 7 or 8 inches high, slender build, high forehead, black hair, black eyes, and wears a heavy black moustache.

JOHN H. SURRATT is about 5 feet 9 inches. Hair rather thin and dark, eyes rather light, no beard. Would weigh 145 or 150 pounds. Complexion rather pale and clear, with color in his cheeks. Wore light clothes of fine quality. Shoulders square, cheek bones rather prominent, chin narrow, ears projecting at the top, forehead rather low and square, but broad. Parts his hair on the right side; neck rather long. His lips are firmly set. A slim man.

DANIEL C. HARROLD is 22 years of age, 5 feet 6 or 7 inches high rather round shouldered, otherwise light built, dark hair (little if any) moustache, dark eyes — weighs about 140 pounds.

GEO. F. NESBITT & CO., Printers and Stationers, cor. Pearl and Pine Streets, N. Y.

John Wilkes Booth, a member of a celebrated theatrical family, was an ardent supporter of the Southern cause. An 1864 attempt by Booth and associates to kidnap Lincoln failed. In 1865 they planned attacks on Vice-President Andrew Johnson and Secretary of State William Seward as well as the president and Seward was stabbed (but not fatally) at about the same time Booth attacked Lincoln. Of the eight conspirators implicated in the plot, four were executed, one fled the country, two were given prison sentences of life, and the last received a prison term of six years. Booth died in a Virginia barn, shot by pursuing army troops thirteen days after the assassination.

The New-

VOL. XIV......NO. 4230.

NEW-YORK, S.

AWFUL EVENT.

President Lincoln Shot by an Assassin.

The Deed Done at Ford's Theatre Last Night.

THE ACT OF A DESPERATE REBEL

The President Still Alive at Last Accounts.

No Hopes Entertained of His Recovery.

Attempted Assassination of Secretary Seward.

DETAILS OF THE DREADFUL TRAGEDY.

[OFFICIAL.]

WAR DEPARTMENT,
WASHINGTON, April 15—1 30 A. M. }

Maj.-Gen. D.x :

This evening at about 9:30 P. M., at Ford's Theatre, the President, while sitting in his private box with Mrs. LINCOLN, Mrs. HARRIS, and Major RATHBURN, was shot by an assassin, who suddenly entered the box and approached behind the President.

The assassin then leaped upon the stage, brandishing a large dagger or knife, and made his escape in the rear of the theatre.

The pistol ball entered the back of the President's head and penetrated nearly through the head. The wound is mortal. The President has been insensible ever since it was inflicted, and is now dying.

About the same hour an assassin, whether

box, waving a long dagger in his right hand, and exclaiming "*Sic semper tyrannis,*" and immediately leaped from the box, which was in the second tier, to the stage beneath, and ran across to the opposite side, making his escape amid the bewilderment of the audience from the rear of the theatre, and, mounting a horse, fled.

The screams of Mrs. LINCOLN first disclosed the fact to the audience that the President had been shot, when all present rose to their feet, rushing toward the stage, many exclaiming "Hang him! hang him!"

The excitement was of the wildest possible description, and of course there was an abrupt termination of the theatrical performance.

There was a rush toward the President's box, when cries were heard: "Stand back and give him air." "Has any one stimulants." On a hasty examination, it was found that the President had been shot through the head, above and back of the temporal bone, and that some of the brain was oozing out. He was removed to a private house opposite to the theatre, and the Surgeon-General of the army, and other surgeons sent for to attend to his condition.

On an examination of the private box blood was discovered on the back of the cushioned rocking chair on which the President had been sitting, also on the partition and on the floor. A common single-barreled pocket pistol was found on the carpet.

A military guard was placed in front of the private residence to which the President had been conveyed. An immense crowd was in front of it, all deeply anxious to learn the condition of the President. It had been previously announced that the wound was mortal; but all hoped otherwise. The shock to the community was terrible.

The President was in a state of syncope, totally insensible, and breathing slowly. The blood oozed from the wound at the back of his head. The surgeons exhausted every effort of medical skill, but all hope was gone. The parting of his family with the dying President is too sad for description.

At midnight, the Cabinet, with Messrs. SUMNER, COLFAX and FARNSWORTH, Judge CUR-

Department and two male nurses, dis them all, he then rushed upon Secretary, who was lying in b the same room, and inflicted stabs in the neck, but severing, thought and hoped, no arteries, he bled profusely.

The assassin then rushed down mounted his horse at the door, and ro before an alarm could be sounded, and same manner as the assassin of the dent.

It is believed that the injuries of th retary are not fatal, nor those of either others, although both the Secretary an Assistant Secretary are very serious jured.

Secretaries STANTON and WELLES other prominent officers of the gover called at Secretary SEWARD'S house to i into his condition, and there heard assassination of the President.

They then proceeded to the house wh was lying, exhibiting of course i anxiety and solicitude. An immense was gathered in front of the Pres house, and a strong guard was also sta there, many persons evidently suppos would be brought to his home.

The entire city to-night presents a sc wild excitement, accompanied by lent expressions of indignation, the profoundest sorrow—many tears. The military authorities dispatched mounted patrols in eve rection, in order, if possible, to arrest sassins. The whole metropolitan poli likewise vigilant for the same purpose.

The attacks. both at the theatre Secretary SEWARD'S house, took place at the same hour—10 o'clock—thus show preconcerted plan to assassinate thos tlemen. Some evidence of the guilt party who attacked the President are possession of the police.

Vice-President JOHNSON is in the cit his headquarters are guarded by troops

ANOTHER ACCOUNT.

Special Dispatch to the New-York Tim

WASHINGTON, Friday. April 1

ugh every body supposes them to have
n rebels.

SATURDAY MORNING –1 O'CLOCK.

he person who shot the President is rep-
ented as about 30 years of age, five feet
e inches in height, sparely built, of light
plexion, dressed in dark clothing, and
ving a genteel appearance. He en-
ed the box, which is known as the State
k, being the upper box on the right
d side from the dress-circle in the regular
nner, and shot the President from behind,
ball entering the skull about in the middle,
ind, and going in the direction of the left
; it did not pass through, but apparently
ke the frontal bone and forced out the
in to some extent. The President is
yet dead, but is wholly insensible, and
Surgeon-General says he cannot live
day-break. The assassin was followed
oss the stage by a gentleman, who sprang
from an orchestra chair. He rushed
ough the side door into an alley, thence
the avenue and mounted a dark bay horse,
ich he apparently received from the hand
an accomplice, dashed up F, toward the back
rt of the city. The escape was so sudden
t he effectually eluded pursuit. The as-
sin cried " sic sempre" in a sharp, clear
ce, as he jumped to the stage, and dropped
hat and a glove.

Two or three officers were in the box with
President and Mrs. LINCOLN, who made
rts to stop the assassin, but were unsuc-
ssful, and received some bruises. The
ole affar, from his entrance into the
x to his escape from the theatre,
cupied scarcely a minute, and the
ongest of the action found everybody
oly unprepared. The assault upon Mr.
WARD appeared to have been made almost
the same moment as that upon the
esident. Mr. SEWARD'S wound is not dan-
rous in itself, but may prove so in connec-
n with his recent injuries. The two
assins have both endeavored to leave the
y to the northwest, apparently not expect-
g to strike the river. Even so low down
Chain Bridge, cavalry have been sent in
ery direction to intercept them.

SATURDAY, 1.30 o'clock A. M.

EUROPEAN NEWS.

TWO DAYS LATER BY THE EUROPA.

The Insult to Our Cruisers by Portugal.

The American Minister at Lisbon Demands Satisfaction.

Dismissal of the Commander of Fort Belan Requested.

Further Advance in Five-Twenties.

FINANCIAL AND COMMERCIAL.

HALIFAX, Friday, April 14.

The steamship Europa, from Liverpool on the
1st, via Queenstown on the 2d inst., arrived here at
2 o'clock this morning. She has 43 passengers for
this port, and 30 for Boston. Her dates are two days
later than those already received.

The steamship Cuba, from New-York, arrived at
Liverpool at noon on the 1st inst.

THE STONEWALL AFFAIR.

A Lisbon dispatch, of the 31st of March, says that
the American Minister at Lisbon has demanded satis-
faction of the Portuguese Government for the firing
upon the Niagara and Sacramento by the Portuguese
forts. He also requests the dismissal of the Com-
mander of Fort Belan, and a salute of twenty-one
guns to the American flag.

Nothing as yet has been decided in regard to the
matter.

A PROPHECY FROM RICHMOND.

The correspondent of the London Times, writing
from Richmond on the 4th of March, says:

" I am daily more convinced that if Richmond
falls and LEE and JOHNSTON are driven from the field,
it is but the first stage of this colossal revolution
which will then be completed. There will ensue a
time when every important town of the South will
require to be held by a Yankee garrison, when exul-
tation in New-York will be exchanged for soberness
and right reason, and when it will be realized that
the closing scenes of this mightiest revolutionary
drama will not be played out, save in the times of our
children's children."

GREAT BRITAIN.

Parliamentary proceedings on the 30th ult.
were unimportant.

In the House of Commons, on the 31st, Lord C.
PAGET said that the Admiralty had received no proposal for sanctioning or supporting any fresh attempt
to reach the North Pole. He was, therefore, unable
to say what course the government would take if
such a proposal were made.

Mr. NEWDEGATE put some questions as to the idea
of the Pope taking up his residence in England, as
indicated in some foreign journals.

Lord PALMERSTON replied that the government re-
spected the Pope personally very much, but for him

omize, but must maintain the position of Austria as
a great Power.

INDIA.

A private Calcutta telegram of March 27 re-
ports commercial affairs in much the same state as
on the 25th, when slight improvement had taken place.

BRAZIL.

LONDON, Sunday, April 2.

The Brazilian mail has reached Lisbon, bring-
ing the following dates:

RIO DE JANEIRO, Saturday, March 11.
Exchange 25⅜ @26¼.
COFFEE.—Sales of good firsts at 65#06. Shipments
100,000 bags. Stock, 100.000 bags. Freights 50#62½.
BAHIA, Saturday, March 11.
Exchange 26¼.
Cotton nominal.
PERNAMBUCO, Saturday, March 11.
Exchange 26½ @27.
Montevideo has surrendered to Gen. FLORES. The
Brazilians now occupy the city.

LATEST VIA LIVERPOOL.

LIVERPOOL, Saturday Evening, April 1, 1865.
The Times to-day has an editorial on the
amended tariff law of the United States. It says:
" It is impossible to find an excuse for it. Tried
by the light of reason or by the results of experience
it is alike condemned."

It ironically credits the framers of the scheme
with peculiar wisdom in selecting the 1st of April
for its inauguration.

The Army & Navy Gazette says: " The work of
the United States Navy has now been accomplished,
and it must be confessed that in the hands of FAR-
RAGUT and PORTER the high reputation which the
officers and seamen of that Power established soon
after the national existence of itself, has been greatly
enhanced."

LATEST VIA QUEENSTOWN.

LONDON, Saturday, April 1.
There is no news of importance this morning.
PARIS, Friday, March 31—P. M.
The Bourse is steady. The Rentes closed at
67f. 30c.

COMMERCIAL.
LIVERPOOL MARKET.

LIVERPOOL, April 31.—Evening.
The Market report was received per Moravian.
COTTON—The stock of Cotton in port is 580.000 bales by
actual count, being 13,000 bales below the estimates, of
which amount 49,000 bales are American.

TRADE REPORT.

The Manchester market was firmer with an upward
tendency.
BREADSTUFFS—The market is easier. Messrs. RICHARD-
SON, SPENCE & Co., and others, report: Flour dull and
easier. Wheat quiet and quotations are barely maintained; red Western 8s. a8s. 8d. Corn inactive; mixed
27s. 6d.
PROVISIONS—The market is downward, WAKEFIELD,
NASH & Co., and others, report: Beef has a downward
tendency. Pork heavy and declined 2s. 6d. Bacon
firmer and holders demand an advance. Lard dull and
easier at 58s. a61s. Butter flat and declining. Tallow
downward.
PRODUCE.—Ashes easier at 23s. 6d. for Pots, and 30s.
for Pearls. Sugar, flat. Coffee, quiet and steady. Rice,
quiet and steady. Clover Seed, firmer. Jute, 10s. @30s.
lower. Cod Oil, quiet at 57s. Sperm Oil, no sales. Linseed Oil, steady. Resin, very dull. Spirits Turpentine,
quiet at 65s. a66s.
PETROLEUM—BOULT, ENGLISH & BRANDON report: Petroleum firm, at 1s. 1¼d. @2s. for refined; no crude in
market.

LONDON MARKETS.

FLOUR firm; WHEAT steady. IRON advancing; bars
and rails, £6 1vs. a£6 15s; Scotch pig, 52s 3d. SUGAR
inactive. COFFEE active at a decline of 1s. @2s. TEA
steady at 10½d. for common Congou. RICE steady.
SPIRITS TURPENTINE firm at 67s. PETROLEUM steady at
£18 for crude, 2s. for refined SPERM OIL nominal at £82.
TALLOW downward at 40s a43s. LINSEED OIL flat.

LATEST COMMERCIAL.

LIVERPOOL, Saturday, April 1—Evening.
COTTON—Sales to-day 6,000 bales, including 2,000 bales
to speculators and exporters. The market is less firm

OUR GREAT LOSS

Death of President Lincoln.

The Songs of Victory Drowned in Sorrow.

CLOSING SCENES OF A NOBLE LIFE.

The Great Sorrow of an Afflicted Nation.

Party Differences Forgotten in Public Grief.

Vice-President Johnson Inaugurated as Chief Executive.

MR. SEWARD WILL RECOVER.

John Wilkes Booth Believed to be the Assassin.

Manifestations of the People Throughout the Country.

OFFICIAL DISPATCHES.

WAR DEPARTMENT, WASHINGTON, }
April 15—4:10 A. M. }

To Major-Gen. Dix:

The President continues insensible and is sinking.

Excerpts from the April 16, 1865 edition of *The New York Times*, giving a minute-by-minute account of the "Awful Event" announced on Saturday.

CLOSING SCENES.

Particulars of His Last Moments—Record of His Condition Before Death—His Death.

WASHINGTON, Saturday, April 15—11 o'clock A. M.

The *Star* extra says:

"At 7:20 o'clock the President breathed his last, closing his eyes as if falling to sleep, and his countenance assuming an expression of perfect serenity. There were no indications of pain, and it was not known that he was dead until the gradually decreasing respiration ceased altogether.

Rev. Dr. GURLEY, of the New-York-avenue Presbyterian Church, immediately on its being ascertained that life was extinct, knelt at the bedside and offered an impressive prayer, which was responded to by all present.

Dr. GURLEY then proceeded to the front parlor, where Mrs. LINCOLN, Capt. ROBERT LINCOLN, Mrs. JOHN HAY, the Private Secretary, and others, were waiting, where he again offered a prayer for the consolation of the family.

The following minutes, taken by Dr. ABBOTT, show the condition of the late President throughout the night:

11 o'clock—Pulse 44.
11:05 o'clock—Pulse 45, and growing weaker.
11:10 o'clock—Pulse 45.
11:15 o'clock—Pulse 42.
11:20 o'clock—Pulse 45; respiration 27 to 29.
11:25 o'clock—Pulse 42.
11:32 o'clock—Pulse 48, and full.
11:40 o'clock—Pulse 45.
11:45 o'clock—Pulse 45; respiration 22.
12 o'clock—Pulse 48; respiration 22.
12:15 o'clock—Pulse 48; respiration 21—echmos both eyes.
12:30 o'clock—Pulse 45.
12:32 o'clock—Pulse 60.
12:35 o'clock—Pulse 66.}
12:40 o'clock—Pulse 69; right eye much swollen, and echmoses.
12:45 o'clock—Pulse 70.
12:55 o'clock—Pulse 80; struggling motion of arms.
1 o'clock—Pulse 86; respiration 30.
1:30 o'clock—Pulse 95; appearing easier.
1:45 o'clock—Pulse 86—very quiet, respiration irregular.

Mrs. LINCOLN present.

2:10 o'clock—Mrs. LINCOLN retired with ROBERT LINCOLN to an adjoining room.
2:30 o'clock—President very quiet—pulse 54—respiration 28.
2:52 o'clock—Pulse 48—respiration 30.
3 o'clock—Visited again by Mrs. LINCOLN.
3:25 o'clock—Respiration 24 and regular.
3:35 o'clock—Prayer by Rev. Dr. GURLEY.
4 o'clock—Respiration 26 and regular.
4:15 o'clock—Pulse 60—respiration 25.
5:50 o'clock—Respiration 28—regular—sleeping.
6 o'clock—Pulse failing—respiration 28.
6:30 o'clock—Still failing and labored breathing.
7 o'clock—Symptoms of immediate dissolution.
7:22 o'clock—Death.

Immediately after the President's death a Cabinet meeting was called by Secretary STANTON, and held in the room in which the corpse lay. Secretaries STANTON, WELLES and USHER, Postmaster-General DENNISON, and Attorney-General SPEED, were present. The results of the conference are as yet unknown.

THE ASSASSINATION.

Additional Details of the Lamentable Event

WASHINGTON, Saturday, April 15.

The assassin of President LINCOLN left behind him his hat and a spur.

The hat was picked up in the President's box and has been identified by parties to whom it has been shown as the the belonging to the suspected man, and accurately described as the one belonging to the suspected man by other parties, not allowed to see it before describing it.

The spur was dropped upon the stage, and that also has been identified as the one procured at the stable where the same man hired a horse in the evening.

Two gentlemen who went to the Secretary of War to apprize him of the attack on Mr. LINCOLN met at the residence of the former a man muffled in a cloak, who, when accosted by them, hastened away.

It had been Mr. STANTON's intention to accompany Mr. LINCOLN to the theatre, and occupy the same box, but the press of business prevented

It therefore seems evident that the aim of the plotters was to paralyze the country by at once striking down the head, the heart and the arm of the country.

FROM RICHMOND.

WASHINGTON, Saturday, April 15.

The Richmond *Whig* of yesterday, contains the following:

HEADQUARTERS DEPARTMENT OF VIRGINIA. }
RICHMOND, Va., April 13, 1865. }

Owing to recent events, the permission for the reassembling of the gentlemen recently acting as the Legislature of Virginia, is rescinded. Should any of the gentlemen come to the city under the notice of reassembling already published, they will be furnished passports to return to their homes. Any of the persons named in the call signed by J. A. CAMPBELL and others, who are found in the city, twelve hours after the publication of this notice, will be subject to arrest, unless they are residents of this city.

E. O. C, ORD, Maj.-Gen.,
Commanding the Department.

NEW YORK CITY.

Proclamation by the Mayor.

MAYOR'S OFFICE, NEW-YORK, April 15, 1865.

Citizens of New York;

The death of the President of the United States may well excite your profound grief and amazement. I respectfully recommend that business be suspended, and that a public mourning for the departed Chief Magistrate be observed throughout the city.

C. GODFREY GUNTHER, Mayor.

The Theatres.

Dispatches from Boston announce that all the theatres in that city will be closed until further notice.

In this city a movement of the same kind has been inaugurated. Fox's Old Bowery Theatre will be closed this evening.

WE CHERISH HIS MEMORY.

A NEATLY PRINTED

Mourning Envelope

With the above excellent Likeness of

OUR BELOVED DEPARTED,

IS NOW READY FOR THE TRADE.

Orders may be sent to S. O. THAYER, over Boylston market, Boston; or to B. B. RUSSELL & Co., No. 55 Cornhill, Boston.

☞ All orders by Mail, Express, or Telegraph, promptly responded to.

Advertisement for memento of Lincoln's funeral.

Lincoln's Funeral

WE MOURN A FATHER SLAIN.

ROUTE.

The Procession will form on Broad Street, the left resting on Fitzwater Street, facing west, and move by the following route:—Up Broad to Walnut, up Walnut to Nineteenth, up Nineteenth to Arch, down Arch to Fifth, down Fifth to Walnut, and thence to the gate in Independence Square.

A. W. AUNER'S PRINTING OFFICE,
N. E. COR. ELEVENTH & MARKET STS., Philada.

In Philadelphia and elsewhere the funeral route was announced by printed cards distributed in advance so the public could witness the procession.

At New York City the funeral railway car was floated across the Hudson River on a special barge with spars, mast, and rigging wrapped with black crepe.

Lincoln's death was deeply mourned by the entire nation. Cities and villages throughout the country competed in the use of black crepe and mourning banners; solemn marches and other impressive funereal displays were the order of the day. After lying in state in Washington, first at the White House and then in the Capitol Rotunda, his body was borne toward Springfield in a special railway car for interment in Oak Ridge Cemetery. The funeral procession made stops at each place where Lincoln had spoken on his inaugural trip from Springfield to Washington in 1861. On May 3, 1865 Lincoln was laid to rest.

A succession of photographs taken in front of Lincoln's Springfield house recorded the presence of the innumerable mourners who wanted keepsakes of the occasion.

Public grief in Chicago culminated in a funeral arch through which the bier passed accompanied by a procession of women in white.

A special committee issued elaborately worded invitations to the final ceremonies in Springfield's Oak Ridge Cemetery. This one (with spelling error) was addressed to Horace Greeley, editor and publisher of the New York *Tribune*. One member of the committee was Lincoln's last law partner, William H. Herndon.

Springfield, Illinois, April 21, 1865.

Hon Horace Greely New York.

While fully realizing the National character of the occasion, the relatives and personal and loving friends and neighbors of our late lamented Chief Magistrate of the United States have deemed it not inappropriate to instruct us to express to you an earnest hope that you may join with them in paying the last earthly tribute of respect to his mortal remains, to be deposited, with appropriate ceremonies, in their final resting place, in this City.

Very respectfully,

JESSE K. DUBOIS,	O. M. HATCH,
O. H. MINER,	SHARON TYNDALE,
JOHN P. REYNOLDS,	W. H. HERNDON.
BENJ. S. EDWARDS,	WILLIAM JAYNE,
GEO. M. BRINKERHOFF,	H. G. REYNOLDS,
JAMES H. BEVERIDGE,	THOMAS J. DENNIS,
COL. A. SCHWARTZ,	ROBERT RUDOLPH,
GEORGE W. SHUTT,	M. K. ANDERSON,
B. F. STEVENSON.	

Committee.

Burial Places of the Lincolns

Abraham Lincoln, grandfather and namesake of the president, was massacred by Indians in May 1786. He is buried at Long Run Cemetery, Jefferson County, Kentucky.

Bathsheba (sometimes spelled Bersheba) Lincoln, grandmother, is probably buried at the Mill Creek Cemetery, Hardin County, Kentucky. The exact date of her death is unknown.

Thomas Lincoln Jr., infant brother, is buried at the Redmond family burial ground near the Knob Creek, Kentucky Lincoln farm located about seven miles north of Hodgenville. Tradition has it that Thomas lived only long enough to receive his name.

Nancy Hanks Lincoln, mother, is buried in Spencer County, Indiana on the grounds of Lincoln Boyhood National Memorial. She died October 5, 1818.

Sarah Lincoln, older sister, lies buried at the Little Pigeon Church Cemetery located approximately one mile south of the Lincoln's Indiana home. Her gravestone bears the inscription: Sarah Lincoln/wife of Aaron Grigsby/ February 10, 1807/January 20, 1828.

Thomas and Sarah Bush Lincoln, father and stepmother, are buried in Gordon Cemetery at Shiloh Church, near Farmington, Illinois in Coles County.

Abraham Lincoln, Mary Todd Lincoln, and their sons Edward, William, and Thomas are buried at Abraham Lincoln Tomb, Oak Ridge Cemetery, Springfield, Illinois.

Robert Todd Lincoln, oldest son, and the only child to reach maturity, lies in the Arlington National Cemetery. He died July 26, 1926. Robert served as secretary of war under two presidents and was a United States minister to Great Britain.

Lincoln Tomb, Oak Ridge Cemetery, Springfield, Illinois.

57

Admirers sent gifts to the president in the nineteenth century—just as they do today. This elkhorn chair, photographed by Mathew Brady in 1864, was presented to Lincoln by an Arizona hunter.

Trivia

Abraham Lincoln's ancestors came from Norfolk County, England near a small town called Hingham.

*   *   *

Lincoln's face was the delight of photographers. He sat for thirty-one different cameramen on sixty-one occasions. There are 119 separate photographs of Lincoln, 39 beardless, 80 with beard. The smallest photograph of Lincoln measures about one-eighth of an inch in diameter, the largest about 18½ by 20⅜ inches. Only 24 pictures were taken out of doors. Ninety-four of the poses are seated. Twenty-four are standing, and one is recumbent in death. Two Washington, D.C. photographers, Mathew Brady and Alexander Gardner, took the majority of Lincoln photographs.

*   *   *

Lincoln was the first president born beyond the boundaries of the original thirteen states.

*   *   *

Some of Lincoln's favorite foods were corn cakes, gingerbread, and burnt sugar cakes.

*   *   *

Lincoln attended five schools as a boy. Two of his teachers were named Zachariah Riney and Caleb Hazel.

*   *   *

Abraham Lincoln never officially affiliated himself with any orthodox church. He did, however, attend church regularly and served as sexton to the Little Pigeon Baptist Church while living in Indiana.

*   *   *

On September 9, 1836 Lincoln was licensed to practice law in the Illinois courts by two Supreme Court justices.

*   *   *

There is no original group photograph showing all the members of the Lincoln family. Photographs of the Lincoln family seen today are composite pictures or reproductions of paintings.

Abraham Lincoln, measuring six feet four inches, was two inches taller than George Washington.

* * *

The first presidential candidate of the Republican party was not Abraham Lincoln in 1860 but John C. Freemont in 1856.

* * *

As a presidential candidate, Abraham Lincoln did not make a single campaign speech advocating his election in either the 1860 or 1864 contests.

* * *

Abraham Lincoln was the first Kentucky-born president.

* * *

On March 2, 1861, two days before his inauguration, a New York newspaper announced that Abraham Lincoln was growing a beard.

* * *

The first political appointment Abraham Lincoln made as president was that of one of two private secretaries, John George Nicolay.

Abraham Lincoln was the first American to have his portrait appear on a United States coin. The Lincoln penny was put into circulation in 1909, during the centennial of his birth.

* * *

Lincoln's second inauguration was the first in which blacks participated.

* * *

Although exempt from the draft because he was commander-in-chief of the army, the president was represented by a substitute in the Union army, J. Summerfield Staples.

* * *

There were five former presidents of the United States living in 1861, the year Lincoln assumed the office of president—Martin Van Buren (died 1862), John Tyler (died 1862), James Buchanan (died 1868), Franklin Pierce (died 1869), and Millard Fillmore (died 1874).

* * *

When Lincoln delivered the Gettysburg Address on November 18, 1863, he may have been suffering from a mild case of smallpox.

A. LINCOLN,

Attorney and Counsellor at Law,

SPRINGFIELD, ILL.

TO WHOM IT MAY CONCERN

My old customers and others are no doubt aware of the terrible time I have had in *crossing the stream*, and will be glad to know that I will be back on the same side from which I started on or before the 4TH OF MARCH next, when I will be ready to *Swap Horses, Dispense Law, Make Jokes, Split Rails*, and perform other matters in a SMALL way.

When Congressman Lincoln left Washington in 1849, he returned to Springfield and his law practice. This undated notice may have been published then as a serious advertisement, but the allusions to Lincoln's style, background, and height also suggest that it originated as a practical joke.

Over 100,000 people contributed to the fund for building the Lincoln National Birthplace Memorial at Hodgenville, Kentucky. An original one-room Kentucky cabin from the early nineteenth century has been reconstructed inside.

Abraham Lincoln was assassinated on a Good Friday.

* * *

The clothing worn by President Abraham Lincoln the night of his assassination is exhibited in Ford's Theatre Museum. In the twentieth century, the Brooks Brothers suit was purchased for $25,000 by the American Trucking Association and given to the museum.

* * *

There were three doctors at Ford's Theatre the evening Lincoln was shot. Dr. Charles A. Leale was the doctor who first rendered medical treatment to the stricken president. Altogether sixteen physicians were at Lincoln's bedside at the time of death.

* * *

Lincoln was the first president to be assassinated.

* * *

The contents of Abraham Lincoln's pockets at the time of his assassination were one pair of gold-rimmed spectacles, one pair of folding spectacles in a silver case, one ivory pocket knife, one fancy watch fob, one large white Irish linen handkerchief, one initialed sleeve button, and one brown leather wallet containing a five dollar Confederate note and nine newspaper clippings.

* * *

* * *

George A. Atzerodt, David E. Herold, Lewis Payne, and Mrs. Mary E. Surratt were tried as suspects in the murder of Abraham Lincoln, and on June 30, 1865 they were sentenced "to be hanged by the neck until dead." The sentence was carried out on a scaffold in a penitentiary yard on July 7.

* * *

Lincoln was the first deceased president to rest in state in the United States Capitol Rotunda.

According to the custodians of the Lincoln tomb, the remains of Abraham Lincoln have been moved seventeen times since the body was placed in a receiving vault in Oak Ridge Cemetery at Springfield, Illinois on May 4, 1865. Construction of the temporary vault, erection of the Lincoln Monument, an attempt to steal the body, and numerous reconstructions of the Springfield memorial are largely responsible for the many secret movements of the Lincoln corpse. The casket was opened five times: December 21, 1865, September 19, 1871, October 9, 1874, April 14, 1887, and September 26, 1901. On November 7, 1876, Terrance Mullen and Jack Hughes attempted to steal Abraham Lincoln's corpse.

Abraham Lincoln's body is enclosed in a lead casket surrounded by a cedar case which rests in a marble sarcophagus.

* * *

Lincoln's funeral train traveled 1,162 miles from Washington, D.C. through Maryland, Pennsylvania, New Jersey, New York, Ohio, Indiana, and Illinois.

* * *

At his death, Lincoln's estate was valued at $110,294.62.

* * *

Abraham Lincoln is buried in a vault ten feet below ground. The vault is steel and concrete, hermetically sealed, topped with twenty inches of concrete.

Memory Check

Directions: Check your memory skills by completing the questions below.

1. Lincoln had three law partners. They were _____, _____, and _____.
2. Abraham Lincoln was assassinated by _____ _____ _____.
3. Abraham was a captain during the _____ _____ War.
4. Lincoln's opponent, Stephen Douglas, was known as the "_____ _____."
5. Abraham and Mary had _____ sons.
6. _____ was the only Lincoln son to reach adulthood.
7. Lincoln was assassinated while watching a play at _____ _____.
8. On February 9, 1809, Abraham was born in a cabin near _____, Kentucky.
9. In 1860, Abraham Lincoln ran for President as a member of the _____ Party.
10. Abraham Lincoln's tomb is located in _____ _____ Cemetery.

True or False

1. Lincoln, his father, and his grandfather were all born in different states.
2. Lincoln lived in Illinois for over 30 years.
3. Lincoln was successful every time he ran for political office.
4. George Washington was taller than Abraham Lincoln.
5. Two of Lincoln's sons died before Abraham.
6. Lincoln was assassinated while his stepmother was still living.
7. Abraham Lincoln married Martha Todd.
8. Abraham Lincoln's mother died from cholera.
9. Abraham Lincoln was the first President with a beard.
10. Mr. and Mrs. Lincoln were watching the play "Our American Cousin," when he was assassinated.

Word Search

Mary Todd, Nancy Hanks, Gettysburg, Stephen Douglas, Hodgenville, Springfield, Washington DC, Robert, Eddie, Tad, Sarah Bush, John Wilkes Booth, Kentucky, Indiana, Thomas, Willie, New Salem, Illinois, Fort Sumter, Appomattox

C	A	E	A	N	J	O	H	N	W	I	L	K	E	S	B	O	O	T	H
D	B	F	P	M	P	B	O	A	C	R	D	M	N	B	C	L	U	H	S
S	T	E	P	H	E	N	D	O	U	G	L	A	S	A	W	T	A	O	V
A	S	D	O	S	F	A	G	G	H	I	J	R	K	D	M	B	I	M	K
R	R	D	M	H	L	N	E	M	G	N	O	Y	P	E	C	D	J	A	E
A	W	I	A	T	R	C	N	S	E	T	U	T	Z	N	E	Y	F	S	N
H	H	E	T	R	B	Y	V	V	T	Y	R	O	B	E	R	T	G	H	T
B	T	H	T	U	W	H	I	X	T	S	J	D	Z	K	L	A	T	N	U
U	I	B	O	Q	F	A	L	G	Y	P	K	D	R	S	P	D	U	E	C
S	O	R	X	X	H	N	L	I	S	R	W	I	L	L	I	E	Z	W	K
H	Q	L	P	A	Q	K	E	R	B	I	L	L	I	N	O	I	S	S	Y
Z	U	M	P	C	L	S	V	W	U	N	K	M	J	I	P	Q	Y	A	S
B	N	P	I	R	Y	M	E	B	R	G	L	X	B	A	C	O	E	L	U
M	O	H	E	W	A	N	O	V	G	F	O	R	T	S	U	M	T	E	R
O	X	N	E	H	F	N	Y	Z	A	I	N	D	I	A	N	A	R	M	R
R	S	L	C	D	D	W	H	A	I	E	Q	C	H	D	O	R	S	I	O
F	H	T	O	B	G	X	O	N	E	L	P	T	E	B	O	G	C	E	T
W	A	S	H	I	N	G	T	O	N	D	C	F	A	C	S	M	O	Y	H

Crossword Puzzle

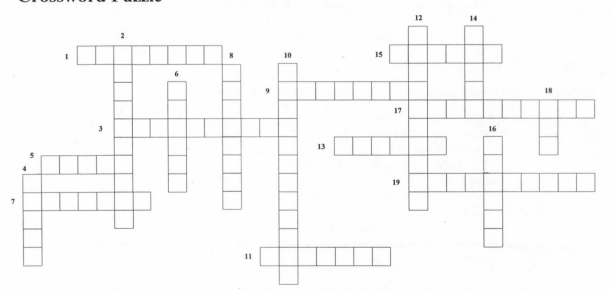

Across

1. Lincoln was born here.
3. Lincoln's political party.
5. First son to die.
7. Second state Lincoln lived in.
9. Abraham married_____.
11. Lincoln debated with him.
13. Lincoln's third son.
15. Only adult son of Abraham and Mary.
17. First battle of the Civil War.
19. Peace was declared here.

Down

2. Lincoln road a flatboat to this city.
4. Stephen Douglas was the "Little_____."
6. Lincoln's first law partner.
8. Fought during Lincoln's Presidency.
10. _____ Proclamation.
12. Lincoln was shot on this holiday.
14. He was a Union General.
16. Lincoln's first Vice-President was Hannibal _____.
18. Youngest son's nickname.

Answers

Word Search

```
C  A  E  A  N  J  O  H  N  W  I  L  K  E  S  B  O  O  T  H
D  B  F  P  M  P  B  O  A  C  R  D  M  N  B  C  L  U  H  S
S  T  E  P  H  E  N  D  O  U  G  L  A  S  A  W  T  A  O  V
A  S  D  O  S  F  A  G  G  H  I  J  R  K  D  M  B  I  M  K
R  W  D  S  H  L  N  M  S  T  U  T  Z  N  E  Y  F  S  A  E
A  H  E  T  R  B  W  H  X  G  T  Y  R  O  B  E  R  T  N  N
H  T  B  Q  W  F  H  A  V  I  T  S  J  D  Z  K  L  A  E  T
B  I  R  X  A  W  N  G  X  T  S  P  K  D  R  S  P  D  W  U
U  O  L  P  Q  H  K  I  R  S  P  W  I  L  L  I  E  Z  S  C
S  Q  M  P  C  L  S  V  W  B  I  I  L  L  I  N  O  I  S  K
H  U  P  I  R  Y  M  E  B  R  N  K  M  J  I  P  Q  Y  A  Y
Z  U  I  R  Y  M  E  B  V  R  G  L  X  B  A  C  O  E  L  S
B  N  R  W  Y  N  O  V  Z  A  F  O  R  T  S  U  M  T  E  R
M  O  E  H  F  N  Y  Z  A  I  N  D  I  A  N  A  R  M  M  R
O  X  N  H  N  N  W  H  I  E  Q  C  H  D  O  R  S  I  I  O
R  S  L  C  D  D  W  H  A  N  L  P  T  E  B  O  G  C  E  T
F  H  T  O  B  G  X  O  N  E  D  C  F  A  C  S  M  O  Y  H
W  A  S  H  I  N  G  T  O  N  D  C  F  A  C  S  M  O  Y  H
```

Crossword Puzzle

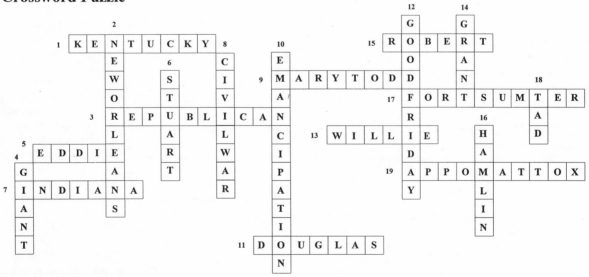

Across:
1. KENTUCKY
3. REPUBLICAN
4. EDDIE
7. INDIANA
9. MARY TODD
11. DOUGLAS
13. WILLIE
15. ROBERT
17. FORT SUMTER
19. APPOMATTOX

Down:
5. GIANT
6. STUART
8. CIVIL WAR
10. EMANCIPATION

Memory Check

1. John Stuart, Stephen Logan, and William Herndon
2. John Wilkes Booth
3. Black Hawk
4. Little Giant
5. Four
6. Robert
7. Ford's Theatre
8. Hodgenville
9. Republican
10. Oak Ridge

True or False

1. True—Kentucky, Virginia, and Pennsylvania
2. True—31 years; from 1830-1861
3. False—He was defeated two times—1832 and 1858
4. False—Lincoln was 6'4" and Washington was 6'2".
5. True—William and Edward
6. True
7. False—Mary Todd
8. False—milk-sickness
9. True—Thanks to Grace Bedell.
10. True—at Ford's Theatre in Washington, DC

Honest Abe Board Game

Rules:

Number of Players: 2 or more players

Materials Needed: Board game attached to book, question list given below, 3 pennies to use as dice, and 1 penny for each player as game tokens. The tokens should each have different mint years.

How to Play: Place player's pennies face down on a flat surface. Each player selects one penny to use as a marker, and places it head up on the Log Cabin Start square.

Player with the lowest mint year on his penny moves first. Player shakes and spills the 3 remaining pennies on a flat surface, and answers a question from the question list. Make sure you cover up the answers! If he is correct, he moves 1 space for each penny turned heads up. If he is incorrect, the player does not advance. If all 3 pennies land head up or tail up, the player may advance 3 spaces without answering a question.

Game ends when 1 player reaches the White House.

Question List

1. Who was the "Little Giant?"
2. Lincoln was shot on this holiday.
3. In what state was Abraham Lincoln born?
4. Name Lincoln's four sons.
5. Name one of Lincoln's three law partners.
6. How did Abraham's father, Thomas, earn a living?
7. True or False: Lincoln's mother died from small pox?
8. True or False: Lincoln was the first President to be assassinated?
9. Name two of Lincoln's jobs.
10. Who died from milk-sickness?
11. Who was Sarah Bush Johnston Lincoln?
12. Who did Lincoln debate in 1858?
13. True or False: Lincoln had two sisters and one brother?
14. Which of Lincoln's sons died at the White House?
15. Who was President of the Confederate States?
16. What did the Emancipation Proclamation do?
17. Which of Lincoln's sons died in their Springfield home?
18. Who assassinated Lincoln?
19. Name Abraham's wife.
20. How was Lincoln's body transported back to Springfield?
21. What war was fought during Lincoln's Presidency?
22. Which son is not buried in the Lincoln tomb in Springfield?
23. True or False: Lincoln grew his beard as a teenager?
24. Who married the Lincolns and later sold them his home?
25. Name the Union General at the peace agreement at Appomattox.
26. Which Lincoln son had a lisp?
27. How tall was Abraham Lincoln?
28. Lincoln was a military captain during what war?
29. True or False: Lincoln was elected as President for one term?
30. How many doctors were present when Lincoln died?

Question Answers

1. Stephen Douglas
2. Good Friday
3. Kentucky
4. Robert, William, Edward, Thomas
5. Stuart, Logan, Herndon
6. Farming, Carpentry
7. False—milk sickness
8. True
9. Surveyor, Store-clerk, Postmaster, Lawyer, Senator, Legislator, President
10. Lincoln's mother
11. Lincoln's stepmother
12. Stephen Douglas
13. False—1 brother, 1 sister, 2 stepsisters, 1 stepbrother
14. William
15. Jefferson Davis
16. Freed the slaves
17. Edward
18. John Wilkes Booth
19. Mary Todd Lincoln
20. By train
21. Civil War
22. Robert
23. False—after he was elected President
24. Rev. Charles Dresser
25. General Grant
26. Thomas
27. 6 feet, 4 inches
28. Black Hawk War
29. False—two terms
30. 16